# 365 Fairy Tales

OM

Om Books International

Published in 2007 by

Om Books International
4379/4B, Prakash House, Ansari Road,
Darya Ganj, New Delhi-110 002
Tel:        91-11-23263363, 23265303
Fax:       91-11-23278091
e-mail:    sales@ombooks.com
           ombooks@bol.net.in
website:   www.ombooks.com

Copyright © Om Books International 2007

Designed and Packaged by: CyberMedia Services
Printed in India by Gopsons Papers Ltd., Noida.

ISBN 10: 8-18710-755-3

ISBN 13: 978 - 8 - 18710 - 755 - 2

# 365
# Fairy Tales

# Contents

*The Story of the Month:    Rapunzel*

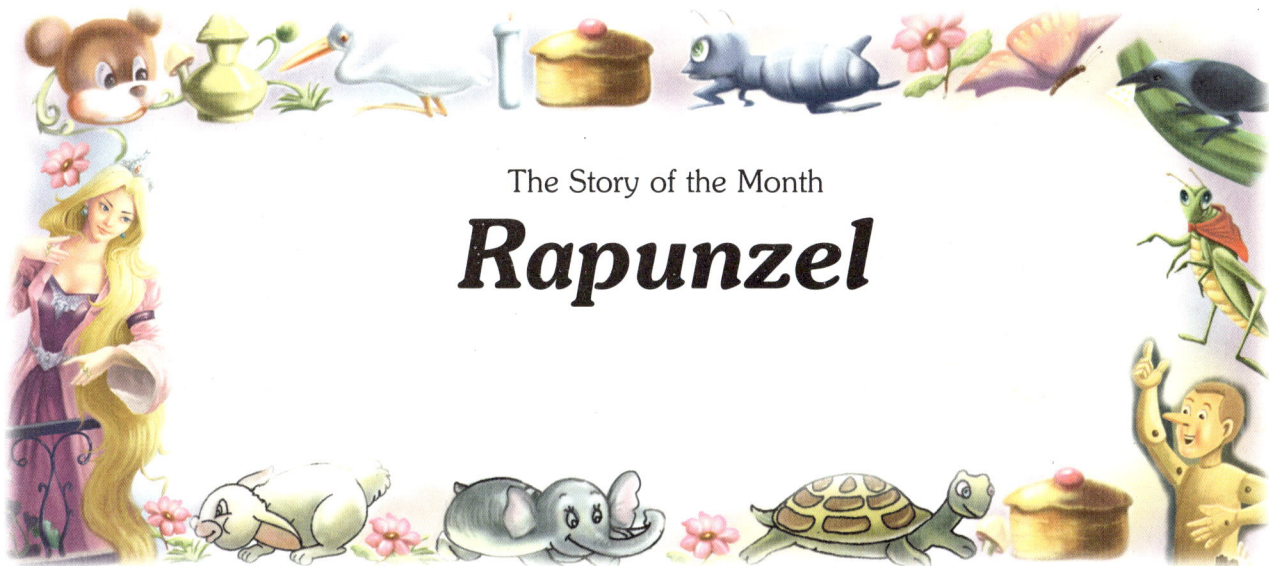

The Story of the Month
# *Rapunzel*

# Rapunzel

Long, long ago in a house that overlooked a beautiful garden lived a childless couple. They prayed to God every day to bless them with a child. One day they found that God had answered their prayer. They were at long last going to have a baby!

Their days passed in happiness but alas! the wife fell ill. She would eat nothing and the husband was worried that she would waste away. He tried to tempt her with many good things but she refused everything. "But you must eat some thing, my dear," he begged her. "There is a herb called Rapunzel in the garden next door. I will feel better if I can eat that," she said. The husband's heart sank when he heard her. This garden was owned by a wicked witch who would let no one enter. But he loved his wife very much and so with a pounding heart, he decided to go into the garden at a time when the witch was away. One day, finding an appropriate time he went into the garden. He had managed to pluck the herb but as he was about to leave, the wicked witch came back. "You thief! How dare you enter my garden?" she screamed. She threatened to put a curse on him. He fell at her feet and begged, "Please don't curse me. If my wife doesn't eat this herb, she will die. She is going to have a baby and is very ill." The witch stopped to think awhile. "I will let you go on one condition. You will give me the baby after it's born." The poor man had no other way out but to agree.

He took the herb to his wife and miraculously she soon recovered and gave birth to a beautiful girl. But as per the agreement the witch came to take the baby away. She took Rapunzel—for that's what she named her—far away and locked her in a high tower. The tower had no doors or

stairs. There was only a window on top.

The only person whom Rapunzel ever saw was the wicked witch. Rapunzel grew up to become beautiful with pretty eyes, a beautiful voice, and her golden hair grew very, very long. All day long, when Rapunzel was alone, she would sing and weep.

Every day, the wicked witch came to the tower with food. She stood at the bottom of the tower and shouted, "Rapunzel! Rapunzel! Let your hair down!" Rapunzel would drop her long, braided hair through the window. The witch

used the hair as a rope to climb into the tower.

One day, a handsome prince was passing by and heard her sing. He fell in love with her voice and unknown to all came to the tower every day to hear her sing. One day, the prince saw the witch climbing up the tower using Rapunzel's hair.

The next day, the prince too called out to Rapunzel. "Let down your hair," he said. The prince climbed to the top of the tower. After that, the prince came to meet Rapunzel every night.

Alas! the witch soon discovered the prince with Rapunzel. She pushed him from the tower onto a thorny bush, making him blind. She banished Rapunzel into the desert far away.

Many years passed. The blind prince wandered alone and finally reached the same desert. One day, he heard familiar voice singing. Following the sound he found her. They hugged each other in joy. Tears of happiness rolled down Rapuzel's cheek. As the tears fell on the prince's eyes, he regained his vision.

The prince took Rapunzel to his kingdom and they lived happily ever after.

## 1 Hansel and Gretel

A poor woodcutter and his wife had two children named Hansel and Gretel. Their mother died when they were young. Hansel and Gretel were very sad. Soon their father remarried but their stepmother was very cruel. One day, she took the children deep into the forest and left them there. Clever Hansel had some breadcrumbs in his pocket and had dropped them on the way so that they could find their way back home. Alas! The birds ate all the crumbs and they couldn't find the path that led back home.

Hansel and Gretel went deeper and deeper into the forest. They were hungry and tired. Finally, after walking for a long time, they saw a cottage made of chocolate, candies, and cake. "Look, Hansel! A chocolate brick!" shouted Gretel in delight and both ate it hungrily.

Now, a wicked witch lived there. When she saw Hansel and Gretel, she wanted to eat them. She grabbed the children and locked them in a cage. The witch decided to make a soup out of Hansel and eat him first. She began boiling a huge pot of water for the soup. Just then, Gretel crept out of her cage. She gave the wicked witch a mighty push from behind and the witch fell into the boiling water. She howled in pain and died instantly. Hansel and Gretel found treasure lying around the cottage. They carried it home with them. Their stepmother had died and their father welcomed them back with tears of joy. They never went hungry again!

## 2 True Love

There lived a king and a queen who wanted a baby. They prayed hard and God finally rewarded them a baby boy. Unfortunately, the baby was born with the head of a donkey. Yet he was well loved because of his sweet nature.

One day, the young prince went to the forest and saw his reflection in a lake. He was very sad, and without telling anyone, left the kingdom. He travelled the world and came to a distant kingdom. Hearing his melodious voice the king of that land made him his court musician. Everyone, even the princess of this kingdom, loved him. She wanted to marry him. The king agreed and celebrated their wedding with great fanfare. At night, when the princess kissed the donkey's head, it fell off from the prince's body. The true love of the princess had broken the spell. And a handsome prince stood in front of the princess. They were very happy and lived happily ever after.

## 3 Rabbits and the Rats

A family of rabbits ran helter-skelter whenever any animal came near them, fearing they would be trampled to death.

One day, hearing the sound of horses' hoof beats from a nearby forest, they were terrified. They decided they would rather die than live in constant fear. So, they went down to the river to drown themselves. When they reached the river, they found lots of mice running hither and thither, to escape their clutches. The rabbits realised that the mice were terrified of them. They were amazed and said, "We thought we were the only little ones who lived in terror. But these tiny animals are even more scared of us."

Happily, they returned to their burrows and stopped living in fear from that day on.

## 4 The Ant and the Grasshopper

In a garden there lived an ant and a grasshopper who were very good friends. It was springtime and the grasshopper was having a lot of fun playing, singing, and dancing in the sun. But the ant was hardworking. It was collecting food grains and storing them in its house.

The grasshopper did not understand why the ant was doing so and said, "Hey, Ant! Why don't you come outside and play with me?" The ant replied, "I cannot. I am storing food for the winter when there won't be anything to eat!" The grasshopper only laughed at the ant and said, "Why are you worrying now? There is plenty of food!" and continued to play, while the ant worked hard.

When winter came, the grasshopper did not find a single grain of food to eat. It began to starve and feel very weak. The grasshopper saw how the hardworking ant had plenty of food to eat and realised its foolishness.

## 5 The Fox and the Crow

One day, a fox saw a crow with a piece of cheese in his beak. The fox was very hungry and thought, "How can I get the piece of cheese?"

He thought for a while. Soon, an idea struck him. He decided to flatter the crow and thus began praising him. He said to the crow, "You are such a pretty and clever bird! If only you could sing as beautifully!"

Now, the crow was very proud. He wanted to show the fox that he could sing very well so he opened his mouth to sing and lo! The piece of cheese he was eating fell to the ground. The fox laughed at the crow and picked up the cheese and ate it hungrily.

Too late the crow realised that one should not be vain.

## 6 The Hare and the Tortoise

A hare met a tortoise walking very slowly towards the market. The proud hare made fun of the slow tortoise. But the tortoise was good-natured and replied, "I may have small feet, but I can beat you in a race." The proud hare laughed and thought, "I can beat him within a second!" So he readily agreed to the race.

The next day, Uncle Elephant, who was the judge of the jungle, began the race by shouting, "Get! Set! Go!" When the hare had covered half of the distance he looked back and saw the tortoise far, far behind. The hare thought, "Let me take a nap. I can run fast and easily win this race!" He sat under a tree and dozed off. When the tortoise passed, he found the hare sleeping.

The hare woke up and realised that the race was already over. The tortoise had reached the end and won the race! The hare was defeated by determination and hard work.

## 7  The Frog Prince

Once upon a time, there lived a beautiful princess who had a golden ball. One day, while playing in the garden, the ball fell into a pond. She was very upset and did not know what to do. While she sat there crying helplessly, a frog hopped out of the pond and asked, "Why are you crying, little princess?" She told him about her golden ball. The ugly frog said, "I can help you get your ball but what will you give me in return?" "I will give you anything you want!" promised the princess. The frog immediately dived into the water and fetched the ball for her. The princess was very happy. The frog reminded her, "Remember that you promised me anything. Well, I want to be your friend, eat from your plate, and sleep in your palace!" The princess hated the idea but she agreed and ran back to the palace.

The next morning, the princess found the frog waiting for her. He said, "I have come to live in your palace." Hearing this, the princess ran to her father, crying. When the kind king heard about the promise, he told her, "A promise is a promise and you must keep your word. You must let the frog stay here." The princess was very angry but she had no choice and let the frog stay. He ate from her plate during dinner and asked the princess to take him to her bed at night. The princess picked him up angrily and threw him to the floor.

In a flash, the frog turned into a handsome prince! He told the princess that he had actually been under the spell of a wicked witch. The princess fell in love with the prince. They were married and lived happily ever after.

## 8  Pinocchio

Gepetto was a poor carpenter who made his living by making puppets. Once, he was carving a puppet out of wood in his workshop. Suddenly the wood squealed, "Ouch! That hurt!" The puppet was alive! Gepetto named the puppet, Pinocchio. Pinocchio wanted to be like other boys and go to school. Gepetto sold his coat to send him to school. One day, on his way to school Pinocchio saw a puppet show in progress. He longed to see it but the ticket cost four pence. Pinocchio sold his books to get the money. He joined the puppets on stage and decided to stay with them. Later that day, Giovanni the puppet master, a fearsome-looking man, needed wood for the fire. He chose Pinocchio as firewood. Pinocchio begged and pleaded to be spared, telling him about his poor father. Giovanni gave Pinocchio five gold coins to give to his father to buy a coat. Gratefully taking the coins, Pinocchio said goodbye to Giovanni and his puppet friends and set off for home.

## 9 Clever Onkie

A rabbit called Onkie lived in the deep African jungles. He was a very intelligent rabbit but Onkie wanted to become even wiser.

So, one day, he went to meet the good witch who lived in the woods. The witch heard Onkie's wish and said, "We shall see! But first bring me a live python!"

Onkie, the rabbit cut the largest branch of a nearby tree and went to the python. He called out, "Pithy, pithy, python, so small like a twig!" The python became very angry and said, "I am not as tiny as you think!" Onkie challenged the python and said, "Then stretch along this branch! Let me measure how big you are!" The python wanted to prove Onkie wrong and did as he was told. As soon as the python stretched himself, the clever rabbit at once tied him to the branch. He went to the witch who was very happy to see it. But she decided to give him another test.

"Bring me a swarm of bees!" she said. Onkie thought of a clever plan. He emptied a pumpkin, put some honey in it, and hung it on a branch. Within a few minutes, it was filled with bees. Onkie quickly closed the opening of the pumpkin and took it to the witch. The good witch was very impressed with Onkie.

The clever rabbit had passed all the tests. The witch then put a dark mark between Onkie's ears for people to know that he was very intelligent and clever. Ever since then, all African rabbits have this dark mark between their ears.

## 10 The Stork and the Fox

A clever fox wanted to play a trick on someone. A stork was sitting nearby. He began talking to her and said that he wanted to be her friend. He then invited her for a meal to his home that evening.

When the stork visited his home that evening she was given a saucer filled with soup. The fox had made delicious soup and put it in a saucer knowing the stork would not be able to drink it, as storks have long beaks. But the stork did not say anything. She couldn't eat anything but talked to the fox politely and went home hungry. The next day, she invited the fox for lunch to her house.

The stork made delicious fish. When the fox arrived, the stork served the fish in a pitcher. The fox stared hungrily at the food but he could not taste it. He had a thick snout and couldn't eat from the pitcher. The stork enjoyed the meal while the fox looked on sheepishly and went home hungry.

## 11 The Sun and the Wind

The Sun and the Wind had an argument as to who was stronger. They kept arguing with each other and couldn't make a decision.

Meanwhile, a traveller was passing by. On seeing him, the Wind said, "The one who is able to make the traveller remove his coat is the winner." The Wind decided to try first, and huffed and puffed and blew as hard as it could, but the traveller just drew his coat tightly around him and kept walking on. Finally, the Wind gave up and it was the turn of the Sun to show its might. The sun shone brightly. Gradually, it grew hotter and hotter and the heat was so unbearable that the traveller finally removed his coat.

The Sun proved his strength and was delighted at winning the argument.

## 12 The Oak and the Sugarcane

An oak tree and a sugarcane plant stood in a field. The oak tree was very proud of his height and strength while the sugarcane was humble and just listened quietly when the oak tree boasted about himself.

One day, when a light breeze was blowing, the oak tree jeered at the sugarcane and said, "Oh, sugarcane! You are so small and light that you would be blown away even by the slightest wind. Look at me! I will always stand tall even in the strongest storm!" The sugarcane kept quiet and did not retaliate.

Suddenly, the wind changed direction and became very fierce. A mighty storm struck the fields and went on and on. The sugarcane bent lightly and let the storm pass over him. But the vain oak tree stood tall and tried to fight the storm. The storm was stronger and the oak tree soon broke and fell. He realised that he should not have made fun of the sugarcane.

# 13 Wild Blossom

There lived a girl named Wild Blossom who used to sell flowers during the day. In the evenings, she would bring food for her little brothers. They loved her very much. One day, Wild Blossom was picking some pansies in the woods when she fell ill. She came home early that day and was very sad because she was not able to buy food for her brothers. The gardeners of heaven saw that Wild Blossom was ill and had no food for her brothers. They came at night and watered the flowers with magic water. They took care of her flowers till she became better.

When Wild Blossom recovered and looked at her garden, she saw that the flowers had not wilted but looked even fresher and more beautiful. She wondered who had been so kind to her. Wild Blossom went to the market and found that there were many buyers for her fresh flowers. She returned home with plenty of food and gifts for her brothers.

# 14 The Foolish Farmer

A farmer and his son were carrying their donkey in a wheelbarrow to the market so as not to tire the animal. Seeing them the villagers laughed. "Whoever has seen a man wheeling a donkey?" they said. This worried the farmer who then rode the donkey. Then the people said, "Look at the selfish man! He is sitting on the donkey while his poor son is running behind!" The farmer put his son on the donkey and began to walk. The people said, "Look at that boy! He is making his old father walk while he sits happy!" Now, both the farmer and the son sat on the donkey and went to the market. The people cried, "Look at them! They are so cruel to the animal!" The farmer decided to tie the donkey's legs to a staff and carry it. The frightened donkey struggled to free himself and fell into the river and drowned.

# 15 The Dancing Teapot

A ragman found a badger caught in a trap. Being good at heart, he set it free. The badger was actually an enchanted being. In order to repay the ragman's kindness, the badger turned himself into a beautiful teapot and slipped inside his bag. The ragman was surprised to find the lovely teapot and presented it to the temple priests.

One day, one of the priests heard the teapot cry on being put to boil. Frightened, the priests gave the teapot back to the ragman. At night, the ragman saw that the teapot had changed itself and looked somewhat like a badger. At the teapot's request, he took it to the market nearby where it danced in front of all. Everyone was delighted and started paying the ragman upon seeing such a wonderful sight. When the ragman became very rich, he decided to give the teapot a well-deserved rest. He took it to the temple and requested the priests to look after it.

# 16 King Midas

King Midas was a very greedy king. Even though he was very rich he always craved for more and more.

One day, he called his court magician and commanded, "Find me a spell that can get me more treasures than I already have." The magician said, "Your majesty, I can give you a power that no one else in this world has. Anything that you touch will turn into gold!" The king was delighted with his good fortune. Everything he touched turned into gold. He turned trees, grass, tables, chairs, flowers, and vases into gold. He thought that he must be the richest man in the world.

But in the evening, when he sat down for supper, King Midas was dismayed. His food turned into gold the moment he touched it and he had to go to bed without any food! However, King Midas was too greedy to be sad about it.

The next morning, the king's daughter ran to hug her father. But alas! The minute she kissed him, she turned into a gold statue! King Midas, who loved his daughter very much, was very sad and he ran to the magician for help. He cried, "Please help me, O Magician! I don't want to be rich anymore. I only want my beloved daughter back." The magician changed everything back to normal.

King Midas had learnt his lesson and was never greedy again.

## 17 Unity Is Strength

Once, an old man was very ill and lay dying in his bed. He had four sons who were always fighting with each other. He always worried about them and wanted to teach them a lesson and asked his sons to come to him. When they came, the old man gave them a bundle of sticks and said, "Can you break these sticks?"

The first son tried to break the bundle but nothing happened. He tried very hard and finally gave up. Then it was the turn of the second son to try his luck. He thought it would be an easy task and picked up the sticks easily. He tried his best to break the sticks but nothing happened. Then, the third son tried to break the bundle of sticks, but he couldn't do anything either.

Meanwhile, the youngest son jeered at his brothers and thought they were very incompetent. He thought he was very clever and took one stick at a time and easily broke all of them.

The old father then smiled at his sons and said, "Children, do you understand what happened? It is always easy to break the sticks one by one. But when they are bundled together, none of you could break them. In the same way, you four brothers should always be together. No one will be able to hurt you then." The four brothers realised what their father was trying to teach them and forgot all their enmity and learnt that unity is strength.

From that day onwards, they never fought with each other and lived together in peace and harmony.

## 18 Honest John

John was a poor woodcutter. His axe was most precious to him. One day, he went to the forest to chop some wood. He was sitting on a high branch on the riverside when suddenly there was a strong wind, and his axe slipped and fell into the river.

The poor woodcutter did not know what to do. He sat by the riverside and started crying. Just then, a river fairy appeared before him. She asked him, "Why are you so sad?"

John told her that he had lost his only axe. The fairy dived into the river and brought out a silver axe. She said, "Here is your axe!" But John said, "It's not mine! I can't take it!" The fairy dived again and brought a golden axe. Again John said, "It's not mine!" The fairy now dived and brought the old iron axe. When John saw it, he said excitedly, "This is my axe!"

The fairy was touched by John's honesty and gave him all the three axes. Now John was rich and lived happily ever after.

## 19 The Little Lost Hedgehog

On a bright sunny day, Mrs. Hedgehog and her family of ten young hedgehogs helped each other wash clothes. Then they all sat on the grassy bank to have cool lemonade and biscuits. Mrs. Hedgehog thought, "How lucky I am to have such wonderful children." Suddenly, she realised that Baby Hedgehog was missing. Everyone started looking in the house, in the garden, in the woods, but Baby Hedgehog could not be seen. Mrs. Hedgehog began to cry and the others cried after her. Losing hope, she picked up her hat. But to her astonishment, she found Baby Hedgehog fast asleep inside the hat. All the hedgehogs were happy to find Baby Hedgehog and cheered in joy. Their friends who lived nearby heard the noise and came out to share their joy too.

## 20 The Milkmaid

A young milkmaid would take a pot of milk and sell it in the market nearby and earn money.

One day on her way to the market, while she was carrying a pot full of milk on her head, she began to daydream. She thought, "Today, I will sell this pot of milk and with the money, I will buy some eggs. Soon, the eggs will hatch and the chickens will grow into lovely, fat hens. These hens will lay more eggs and I will sell all the eggs and get more money. I will then buy a cow with that money. That cow will give me buckets and buckets of milk and I will become very rich when I sell the milk. Then I will buy more cows and become richer and richer everyday."

But alas! While the milkmaid was lost in thought, she did not look where she was walking. She tripped on a stone and fell down. The pot broke and sadly she watched all her dreams flow away with the milk.

## 21 Who Will Bell the Cat?

There was a certain cat that was troubling the mice and had killed many of them. All the mice met to talk about this big problem. The mice wanted to get rid of the cat and decided to make a plan. The mice sat and talked for a very long time but could not come to any conclusion.

An old mouse stood up and said, "I know what we should do! We should tie a bell around the cat's neck. When the bell tinkles, we will know where the cat is!" All the other mice liked the idea. But one young mouse stood up and asked, "That is a good idea, but may I ask who will bell the cat?" None of the mice wanted to do that. The young mouse then said, "It is easy to sit and have big ideas. But it is never easy to carry them out."

## 22 The Lion and the Mouse

A little mouse was passing through a lion's den. The lion caught him and was about to smash him when the little mouse spoke, "Sir, please let me go, and I will do you a good turn one day, for sparing my life."

The lion was rather amused to hear this, thinking, "What good can he do me . . ." but he let him go.

Two weeks later, some huntsmen came to the same forest and spread a net around the lion's den. The lion was captured. He struggled hard to set himself free but he soon realised he was trapped. He roared with anger.

The little mouse was looking for food, when he heard the lion's roar. He ran to him. Seeing the lion caught in the net, he started gnawing at it at once. The mouse had sharp teeth and he soon freed the lion.

The lion was very grateful to the little mouse. From that day, they became the best of friends.

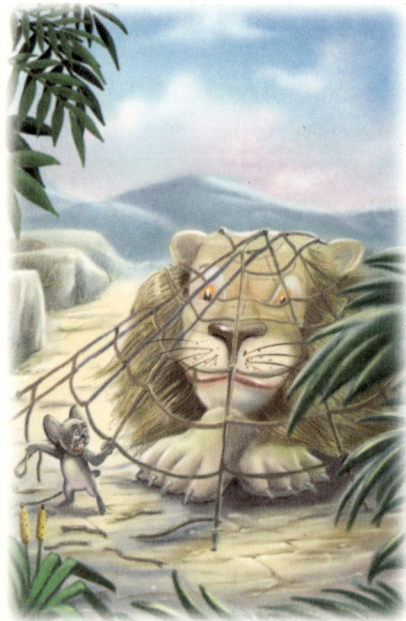

## 23 Queen of Riddles

A clever queen who lived in Petersburg was very vain. "I am good at everything. Isn't there anyone who can beat me?" she thought to herself. One day she announced, "I, the queen, will marry the man who asks me three riddles which I cannot answer." Many people came from far and wide and tried their luck, but failed.

Finally, young Ivan, a peasant from the neighbouring village, came up with three riddles and set off for the queen's palace. He asked the first riddle: "I saw one good thing with another good thing in it. In order to do good, I took the second good thing out of the first good thing."

The queen did not know the answer. She made an excuse saying, "I have a headache," and left. Later in the night, she asked her maidservant to coax out the answer from Ivan. The maid did as she was told. The next day, when Ivan appeared the queen said, "Here's the answer: A horse was in a wheat field and I chased it out."

Ivan asked his second riddle "On the road I saw a bad thing. I took up a second bad thing and hit it. So one bad thing killed another bad thing." The queen again did not know the answer. She sent her maid to coax the answer out of Ivan again. When Ivan came in the morning she said, "I saw a snake on the road and killed it with a stick." Ivan then asked his third riddle. "How did you know the answers to the first two riddles?"

The queen did not want to admit that she had cheated. "I don't know," she replied. Ivan married the queen and they lived happily ever after.

## 24 The Greedy Dog

Once upon a time, there lived a dog. One day, he was very hungry and went in search of food. To his delight, the dog found a juicy bone. The dog happily carried the bone back home. He held the bone tightly in his mouth and scowled at anyone who tried to take it away.

On his way home, he had to cross a bridge. While crossing the bridge, the dog saw his reflection in the water below. The foolish dog thought there was another dog in the water, holding another juicy bone. The greedy dog wanted to have that bone too. He growled and barked at his own reflection in the water. "I'll get that bone too," thought the greedy dog, and he snapped his sharp teeth and barked at his reflection in the water.

But alas! The moment the foolish dog opened his mouth to snap his teeth, the piece of bone fell into the stream. The dog lost his bone and had to go home, hungry.

## 25 The Tulip Fairies

Catrina loved her garden and was very proud of all the flowers. She also had a beautiful bed of tulips in her garden. She watered the garden every day and carefully pulled out weeds that she saw growing. One night she awoke to sounds of lullabies and gurgling babies. She went to her window but could see nothing. The next night she heard the sounds again. This time, she softly crept out to her garden and her eyes widened in amazement. Standing beside each tulip was a fairy mother and inside each tulip-cup was a baby. The babies were laughing and playing as their mothers rocked their tulip beds and tried to sing them to sleep.

From that day on the woman never plucked a tulip or let anyone else touch them. The tulips grew brighter and were in bloom throughout the year. Many people came to see the tulips but the fairies who dwelled there were Catrina's own secret.

## 26 The Fox and the Cockerel

Once, a sly fox got inside a coop and caught Chanti, the cock, by its neck. The other hens squawked with fear on seeing this. The farmer, his wife, and their dogs came running out to see what had happened. Seeing the sly fox, they understood at once what the matter was. Since Chanti was the farmer's most-loved cock, everyone started chasing the fox to rescue him, including the dogs, who kept barking as they ran.

Chanti, who was in the fox's jaws, jeered at him "What kind of a fox are you? They call you names and you don't even reply?"

Insulted by this remark, the fox shouted, "You blockheads, you will never catch me." The moment he opened his mouth, Chanti fell out, and at once flew to the nearest tree. Using its wits, the cock had saved himself.

## 27 The Two Friends

Two friends talked and sang merrily as they walked through the forest. Suddenly a bear appeared. The first friend quickly climbed a tree. The second one wanted help but his friend had already left him. He was very scared because the bear was big and strong and could easily kill him. He thought hard and when the bear came near, he lay very still on the ground and controlled his breath. The bear came close to him and sniffed and smelt his body all over. Now, bears do not attack the dead. The bear walked away thinking that the man was dead. The first friend then came down from the tree when the bear went away. He asked his friend mockingly, "What did the bear tell you?"

The second friend thought for a while. "The bear told me never to trust a friend who escapes and leaves you alone when you need him most," he said. The first friend realised his mistake and was ashamed of his behaviour.

## 28 Chico and the Crane

There was a cook named Chico. His master had visitors for dinner and Chico was told to fry a crane. Chico felt hungry and so he ate one leg of the crane.

At dinnertime, when the master saw a missing leg, he shouted, "Chico! Why does this crane have only one leg?" Chico replied, "Sir, haven't you seen cranes before? They only have one leg!" To teach Chico a lesson, next morning, his master took him to the pond nearby. Chico exclaimed, "Look, Master! Cranes have only one leg!" The master clapped his hands and all the cranes uncurled their other legs and flew away. "You fool! Did you see they have two legs!" cried the master. Clever Chico replied, "Sir, why didn't you clap your hands at the table? You would have got two legs!"

## 29 The Giant and the Tailor

Once, there lived a tailor who was very proud. He hardly did any work and decided to go abroad and seek his fortune in the world.

On the way he met a big giant. The giant invited him to stay with him provided he searched for food for him. The frightened tailor kept wondering how he could escape from the giant.

When the giant ordered him to fetch a jug of water, the tailor boasted that he could get the whole well. Hearing this, the giant was alarmed. When the giant asked him to get wood, the tailor declared that he could bring the whole forest. The giant, who was actually very timid, was terrified and wanted to get rid of the tailor.

The next day, the giant told him to sit on the branch of a tree and bend it. The tailor drew in his breath so hard that he was hurled high into the air and was never seen again. He had learnt his lesson for being so vain.

## 30 Salem and the Nail

Salem was a carpet trader. Once, his shop caught fire and he lost everything. He was very upset and had no means of earning a living now. He decided to sell his house and buy carpets with that money. However, Salem did something strange. He decided to sell the whole house except for a nail. Abu willingly bought Salem's house. And so, while Abu lived in his new house, Salem would visit him. He would hang his big bag or cloak on the nail. Abu did not mind that at all. One day, Salem dragged in a stinking dead donkey and hung it on the nail! Abu begged him to take it away but Salem refused. It was his nail and he could hang anything he wanted on it. When the stink got really bad, Abu was forced to give the house back to clever Salem and ran away. Salem was rich and happy again.

# 31 Tom Thumb

Once, a farmer and his wife had their first child after many years of marriage. The boy was as small as his father's thumb. The queen of fairies came dancing and named him Tom Thumb.

One day, while Tom's mother was making pudding, Tom, who was playing nearby, slipped inside the bowl and was drowned in the batter. He started kicking and thrashing to save himself. The movement in the pudding scared his mother, who was unable to see Tom inside. She gave the batter away to a beggar, who later discovered little Tom inside. Tom came back from the beggar's house and told his parents all that had happened and his mother felt very sorry for what she had done.

A few days later, a raven picked up little Tom and dropped him in the sea. A magnificent fish swallowed him. After a while, some fishermen caught the fish and gave it to King Arthur's servants. When the servants cut the fish, they were surprised to see Tom inside and presented him to King Arthur. The king was delighted and kept Tom who entertained everyone with his funny tricks. Later, Tom was knighted and became Sir Thomas Thumb.

One day, the queen of fairies took Tom to fairyland but by the time he returned, King Arthur and all his knights had died. Tom stayed with the new king in his palace and continued to entertain everyone with his tricks for a long time to come.

# Contents

*The Story of the Month:   Cinderella*

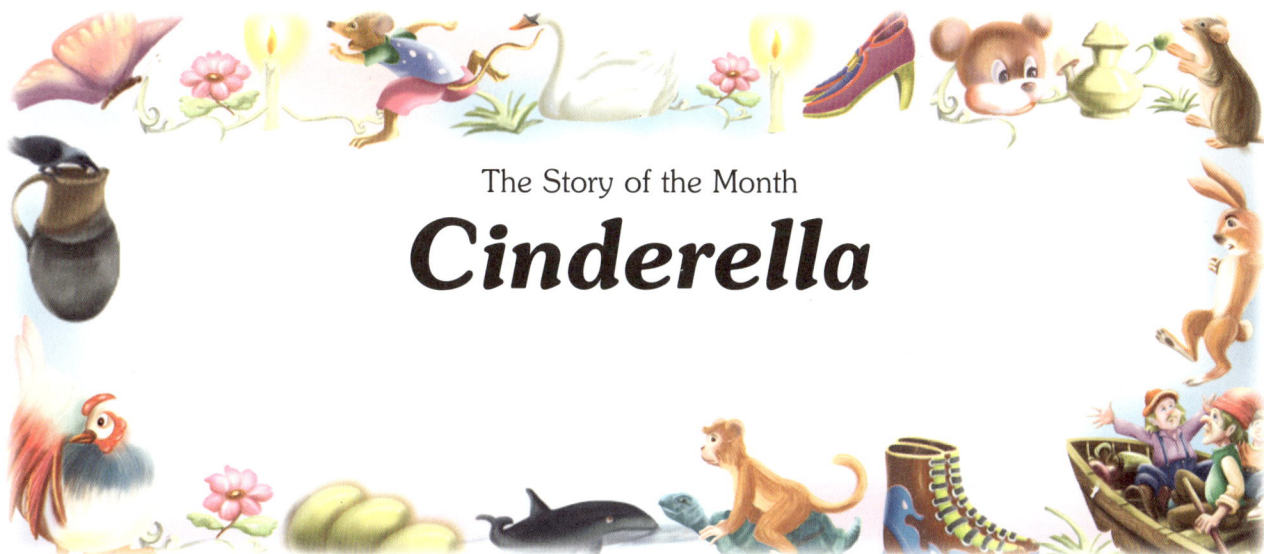

The Story of the Month

# Cinderella

# Cinderella

Once upon a time, there was a beautiful girl named Cinderella. She lived with her wicked stepmother and two stepsisters. They treated Cinderella very badly. One day, they were invited for a grand ball in the king's palace. But Cinderella's stepmother would not let her go. Cinderella was made to sew new party gowns for her stepmother and stepsisters, and curl their hair. They then went to the ball, leaving Cinderella alone at home.

Cinderella felt very sad and began to cry. Suddenly, a fairy godmother appeared and said, "Don't cry, Cinderella! I will send you to the ball!" But Cinderella was sad. She said, "I don't have a gown to wear for the ball!" The fairy godmother waved her magic wand and changed Cinderella's old clothes into a beautiful new gown! The fairy godmother then touched Cinderella's feet with the magic wand. And lo! She had beautiful glass slippers! "How will I go to the grand ball?" asked Cinderella. The fairy godmother found six mice playing near a pumpkin, in the kitchen. She touched them with her magic wand and the mice became four shiny black horses and two coachmen and the pumpkin turned into a golden coach. Cinderella was overjoyed and set off for the ball in the coach drawn by the six black horses. Before leaving, the fairy godmother said, "Cinderella, this magic will only last until midnight! You must reach home by then!"

When Cinderella entered the palace, everybody was struck by her beauty. Nobody, not even Cinderella's stepmother or stepsisters, knew who she really was in her pretty clothes and shoes. The handsome prince also

saw her and fell in love with Cinderella. He went to her and asked, "Do you want to dance?" And Cinderella said, "Yes!" The prince danced with her all night and nobody recognized the beautiful dancer. Cinderella was so happy dancing with the prince that she almost forgot what the fairy godmother had said. At the last moment, Cinderella remembered her fairy godmother's words and she rushed to go home. "Oh! I must go!" she cried and ran out of the palace. One of her glass slippers came off but Cinderella did not turn back for it. She reached home just as the clock struck twelve. Her coach turned back into a pumpkin, the horses into mice and her fine ball gown into rags. Her stepmother and stepsisters reached home shortly after that. They were talking about the beautiful lady who had been dancing with the prince.

The prince had fallen in love with Cinderella and wanted to find out who the beautiful girl was, but he did not even know her name. He found the glass slipper that had come off Cinderella's foot as she ran home. The prince said, "I will find her. The lady whose foot fits this slipper will be the one I marry!" The next day, the prince and his servants took the glass slipper and went to all the houses in the kingdom. They wanted to find the lady whose feet would fit in the slipper. All the women in the kingdom tried the slipper but it would not fit any of them. Cinderella's stepsisters also tried on the little glass slipper. They tried to squeeze their feet and push hard into the slipper, but the servant was afraid the slipper would break. Cinderella's stepmother would not let her try the slipper on, but the prince saw her and said, "Let her also try on the slipper!" The slipper fit her perfectly. The prince recognized her from the ball. He married Cinderella and together they lived happily ever after.

# 1 Amin and the Eggs

Once, there lived a farmer called Amin in Arabia. He lost all his crops due to a drought and became poor. So he asked a trader to lend him a dozen boiled eggs. The next day he set off on his donkey to seek his fortune.

After seven years, Amin came back to his native village a rich man. He rode a fine black horse and had many camels carrying gold and silver. Soon everyone came to know of his wealth. When the greedy trader heard this, he asked for five hundred silver coins as payment for the eggs that he had given to Amin seven years ago. Amin refused to pay. They took the matter to court.

On the day of the hearing, Amin arrived forty minutes late, panting. The judge asked, "Where have you been?" Before Amin could reply, the greedy trader spoke, "Sir, Amin owes me five hundred silver coins. I gave him a dozen eggs. A dozen chickens must have hatched from them. These would have laid even more eggs. I too would have been rich by now." The trader thought that the judge would decide in his favour. "The judge asked Amin again, "Why are you so late?" Amin simply said, "Sir, I was planting a dozen boiled beans in the garden, so that I have a good crop of beans next year."

The judge shouted, "You fool! Since when did boiled beans start growing?" At once Amin replied, "And, sir, since when did boiled eggs start hatching?" Amin won the case while the trader hung his head in shame and walked away.

# 2 The Man and the Trees

A long time ago, there lived a man named Kenny who was very devious and mean. He used to take advantage of the goodness and innocence of others. He wanted to become rich, but did not want to spend his own money.

One day, Kenny went to the forest and asked the trees for some wood. The trees were kind, and thought that Kenny needed some wood to keep himself warm. So they gladly gave him a branch. But Kenny was very wicked. He made an axe out of that wood and began to cut trees down.

Even in their wildest dreams, the trees had never imagined that the wood they had given would be used to make an axe to destroy them. They could not believe that the man to whom they had been so good would be so cruel and chop them down. They felt hurt and cheated but they could not do anything. Unfortunately, they had given Kenny the means to destroy them.

# 3 Country Mouse and Town Mouse

A town mouse decided to visit his cousin in the countryside. They had a wonderful time in the meadows and fields.

After a few days, the town mouse invited his cousin to the town. When the country mouse saw the town mouse's house, he was surprised. There were so many things to eat! While they ate, a woman came into the kitchen and saw the mice. She shrieked so loudly that her husband came running. "It's those mice again! Let me bring the cat in here," he said. Within seconds, a huge black cat chased the mice out of the kitchen. The country mouse said, "Cousin, I am happy that you have so many things to eat, but I would rather live safely in the country eating my simple meals!" Saying this, the country mouse returned home.

# 4 Tutu the Ballerina

Tutu was a ballerina with a pretty frock and dainty little ballet shoes. Wendy, Tutu's owner carried her to all the ballet performances. Tutu enjoyed the performances very much.

But the other toys were jealous of her. They found that though Tutu was dressed like a ballerina she could not really dance. So they started teasing her about it. Tutu was very unhappy. She wanted to be friends with all the other toys.

Suddenly, an idea struck her mind. Though the other toys could not go to the ballet she could bring the stories to them! She gathered them all around her and began telling them the story of *The Swan Lake*.

All the toys listened keenly. Tutu was able to bring the whole performance to life in front of their eyes.

From that day on, whenever Tutu went to a ballet performance, all the toys would be eagerly waiting up for her to listen to her stories.

# 5 The Thirsty Crow

One day a crow was feeling very thirsty. On a hot summer day, she flew here and there in search of water but in vain. She continued to search hard but couldn't find any water to quench her thirst. Then after a long time, she found a pitcher, with a little water in it.

The neck of the pitcher was too long and the water level too low. The crow could not reach the water with her beak. She saw many pebbles around. Suddenly, the crow had an idea. She picked the pebbles one by one and dropped them in the pitcher. And lo! The level of water slowly rose to the top. The crow drank it thirstily. She was very happy.

This story proves that if you try hard enough you can overcome any problem.

# 6 The Pink Elephant's Party

Pink Elephant was new to Toy Town. So she thought, "I shall invite everyone to a party. That way I can make new friends." She went and dropped an invitation in every letterbox. When she returned, she found that the number plates on her gate had fallen. She picked them up and put them back.

Next morning, she decorated her house and cooked lovely things. Then she waited for her guests to arrive. Time passed by but no one came. At last, she stepped out of her house. To her surprise, there were many toys passing by her house with presents in their hands. They said that they were going to Pink Elephant's party. Suddenly, Pink Elephant realised that she had put the numbers on her gate the wrong way. The invitation said house number 13 but the numbers on the gate read 31. Seeing this, everyone laughed and came to the party. Pink Elephant made lots of new friends!

# 7 Goldilocks

Goldilocks was a playful little girl who had lovely golden hair and that is why she was called Goldilocks.

One day, while roaming the woods, she saw a pretty cottage. She went inside and saw three bowls of porridge on the table. Tasting the porridge in the biggest bowl she said, "This porridge is too hot!" She tasted some porridge from the second bowl and said, "This porridge is too cold!" Then tasting some porridge from the third bowl she said, "This porridge is *just* right!" and she ate all of it. After that Goldilocks felt sleepy, so she went upstairs where she saw three beds. She lay on the first bed and said, "This bed is too hard!" She lay on the second bed and said, "This bed is too soft!" Finally, she lay on the third bed and said, "This bed is just right!"

And so, Goldilocks curled up and went to sleep.

The cottage actually belonged to three bears. When they came home in the evening, the three bears saw that someone had been there. Mama and Papa Bear ate their porridge but the little bear wailed, "There is nothing left in my bowl!"

When they went upstairs to sleep, Papa Bear and Mama Bear found their beds had been used. Papa Bear shouted, "Someone has been sleeping in my bed!" Then, Mama Bear cried, "Someone has been sleeping in my bed!" The little bear saw Goldilocks sleeping in his bed and squealed, "Someone is still sleeping in my bed!"

Goldilocks awoke and seeing the three bears, she jumped up in fright and ran out of the door, never to be seen in the woods ever again!

# 8 The Hare and the Porcupines

A porcupine went to the market to buy vegetables. He was walking very slowly as all porcupines do when he met a hare.

The hare made fun of him saying, "Look how slowly you walk!" The porcupine replied, "I am slow, but I can still beat you in a race!" "Fine!" said the hare, " If you win, I will give you a penny!"

The clever porcupine went home and told his brother about the race and they thought of a plan to fool the hare.

The race began and the hare ran as fast as he could. But when he reached the finish line, he found the porcupine waiting for him saying, "Slowpoke! Look how fast I can run!"

The hare had lost the race. He was amazed that the porcupine had won and meekly gave the porcupine a penny. He did not know that there were two porcupines in the race. One had started with him and the other had been waiting at the finish line!

## 9 Sweet Porridge

A poor girl lived alone with her mother. She went to the forest in search of food. There she met an old woman who gave her a little magic pot, which could cook porridge when ordered to.

The girl was very happy and ran all the way home with the pot. Her mother was delighted. They ate as much porridge as they wanted. Now they never had to worry about food. One day, when the girl had gone out, the mother ordered the pot to cook porridge but forgot what to say to stop it from cooking. So the pot went on cooking till the whole house and even the streets were full of porridge. No one knew how to stop it.

The mother sat and cried at the mess but couldn't do anything about it. When the girl returned, she ordered the pot to stop cooking. All those who came to help had to eat their way back to their houses!

## 10 The Spider and the Fly

Spiky the spider fell in love with Daisy the fly. He told her of his love for her and begged her to become his wife. But the Daisy did not like the Spiky and so she refused to marry him. Spiky tried his best to woo the fly but she was not willing to change her mind.

One day, the Daisy saw Spiky coming towards her. She quickly shut the doors and windows of her house and put a pot of water to boil on the fire. She waited for some time and when the spider called out to her, she quickly threw the boiling water at him. Spiky was enraged and cursed the fly, "I will never forgive you. My descendants and I shall always hate you and will never let you live in peace. You will regret this."

That is why even today one sees how spiders hate flies.

## 11 There Is No Doubt about It

A hen pecked herself with her beak and a little feather came out. She said merrily, "The more feathers I pluck, the more beautiful I'll become."

Her neighbour heard this and passed the word to her neighbour. An owl overheard the conversation and related the story to his neighbour adding a few more details himself.

The neighbour flew away to tell the doves, "There is a hen who has plucked her feathers to look good and get the cock's attention."

The doves spread the news further. Finally, the story was that five hens had killed each other for the sake of a cock.

Soon, it reached the first hen's ears. Not realising that it was indeed her own story she passed on the exaggerated story to her neighbours.

In this way the story became very different from the original. There is no doubt; one little feather may easily grow into five hens!

## 12 The Lonely Lighthouse

There stood a little lighthouse in the middle of the sea on top of the rocks. Its light shone far out to sea but no ship had passed by for years. So one day, the lighthouse keeper left it and went away. The lighthouse was very sad at being left all alone. The seals and walruses who lived near the rocks felt sorry for the lonely lighthouse. They decided to take turns at working the light of the lighthouse. This way it would keep shining and not feel lonely. The lighthouse was happy on hearing this.

Since then, every night the lighthouse shone its light and the dolphins, seals, walruses, and even a few whales, came out to play in its light. They all had a wonderful time. With so many friend, the little house was never lonely after that.

# 13 The Lonely Monkey

A little brown monkey lived all by himself on a tiny desert island near the sea. He was very lonely as there was no one to play with him.

One day, a fish who was swimming by, saw the monkey sitting alone in one part of the island and told him to follow him to another island nearby where he could make lots of friends.

The monkey tried to swim but did not like being wet. A pelican tried to teach him to fly but that was too difficult for him. Finally, the monkey decided to chop down all the trees to make a raft. But a turtle hearing him said that it was a silly idea as then there would be nothing left for anyone to eat. The turtle offered to take the monkey on its back across the sea but the monkey was too big for him. Finally, the turtle's great-grandfather carried the monkey on its back to the other island. The monkey was very happy because he found lots of monkeys there and knew that he would never be lonely again.

# 14 Tricking the Devil

There lived a wicked devil who would capture men and set before them tasks that none could do. One day, the devil captured a poor villager. "If you tell me a  job that none can do then I shall pay you a thousand gold coins, but if you cannot then I shall keep you in my prison." The villager was at his wit's end for he knew there was no task that was impossible for the powerful devil.

After a few days the devil again returned but the villager was still unable to think of a job. "Why are you looking so scared?" asked his wife. The man explained everything to his wife. "Give the devil my curly hair and ask him to straighten it!" said his wife with twinkling eyes.

The villager gave the hair to the devil who did everything possible to straighten it, but to no avail. He paid the man and was never seen again.

## 15 The Three Wishes

A poor woodcutter went to the forest to cut wood. He was about to cut an oak tree when a fairy appeared and begged him to spare the tree. The woodcutter was a kind man and did not cut the tree and the grateful fairy granted him three wishes. When he reached home he was hungry. He remembered the fairy and wished for black pudding. At once, he saw a bowl of the finest black pudding in front of him.

The woodcutter told his wife about the fairy but she did not believe him. To test her husband's words, she wished that the pudding would stick on her husband's nose. Suddenly, the pudding stuck on his nose! They tried hard to pull it off but it stuck hard. The woodcutter used his last wish and wished for the pudding to come out. The pudding came off and lay on a dish. So though they had the finest pudding for dinner, they had used up all the wishes.

## 16 The Ugly Duckling

A little duckling was very sad because he thought he was the ugliest amongst all his brothers and sisters. They would not play with him and teased the poor ugly duckling. One day, he saw his reflection in the water and cried, "Nobody likes me. I am so ugly." He decided to leave home and went far away into the woods.

Deep in the forest, he saw a cottage in which there lived an old woman, her hen, and her cat. The duckling stayed with them for some time but he was unhappy there and soon left. When winter set in the poor duckling almost froze to death. A peasant took him home to his wife and children. The poor duckling was terrified of the children and escaped. The ugly duckling spent the winter in a marshy pond.

Finally, spring arrived. One day, the duckling saw a beautiful swan swimming in the pond and fell in love with her. But then he remembered how everyone made fun of him and he bent his head down in shame. When he saw his own reflection in the water he was astonished. He was not an ugly duckling anymore, but a handsome young swan! Now, he knew why he had looked so different from his brothers and sisters. "They were ducklings but I was a baby swan!" he said to himself.

He married the beautiful swan and lived happily ever after.

## 17 Little Red Riding Hood

One day, Little Red Riding Hood's mother said to her, "Take this basket of goodies to your grandma's cottage, but don't talk to strangers on the way!" Promising not to, Little Red Riding Hood skipped off. On her way she met the Big Bad Wolf who asked, "Where are you going, little girl?" "To my grandma's, Mr. Wolf!" she answered.

The Big Bad Wolf then ran to her grandmother's cottage much before Little Red Riding Hood, and knocked on the door. When Grandma opened the door, he locked her up in the cupboard. The wicked wolf then wore Grandma's clothes and lay on her bed, waiting for Little Red Riding Hood.

When Little Red Riding Hood reached the cottage, she entered and went to Grandma's bedside. "My! What big eyes you have, Grandma!" she said in surprise. "All the better to see you with, my dear!" replied the wolf. "My! What big ears you have, Grandma!" said Little Red Riding Hood. "All the better to hear you with, my dear!" said the wolf. "What big teeth you have, Grandma!" said Little Red Riding Hood. "All the better to eat you with!" growled the wolf pouncing on her. Little Red Riding Hood screamed and the woodcutters in the forest came running to the cottage. They beat the Big Bad Wolf and rescued Grandma from the cupboard. Grandma hugged Little Red Riding Hood with joy. The Big Bad Wolf ran away never to be seen again. Little Red Riding Hood had learnt her lesson and never spoke to strangers ever again.

## 18 Ben's New Seat

Ben, a grizzly bear, had no friends and felt lonely in the forest. He decided to make a seat under a tree and watch everyone pass by. In this way, he would be able to make many friends. Next day, Ben sat on his new seat. Soon, a grey rabbit came by. He was very curious to see the seat and hopped onto it merrily. Then a squirrel jumped down from a branch above and sat next to the rabbit. Soon, two raccoons came scampering by and jumped on the seat too. Then a red fox and a stoat came running along and joined them. Now the seat was very crowded. Hearing their noise and laughter, a tiny bluebird also joined them.

But the seat could not take so much weight. It creaked and slowly all the legs broke and everyone fell down laughing. Ben had made so many friends and was very happy. He decided to make a bigger seat, which would be big enough for all his friends.

## 19 The Peasant and the Master

A peasant was talking to his master and other friends. He told them that a mouse had eaten up all his cheese. The master was a rich and proud man. He called the peasant a fool and told him that it was not possible for a mouse to eat cheese. To the peasant's dismay, everybody agreed with the master. He kept silent.

After a little while, the master said he had rubbed his ploughshares with oil to keep them from rusting but the mice had eaten up all the points. Now the peasant broke out. "How is it that the mice ate up the points of your ploughshare but not my cheese?" But the master and all the others silenced him and said that the master was always right. The poor peasant was very upset and couldn't find anybody who would agree with him.

## 20 The Princess and the Pea

A prince who was searching for the perfect wife wanted to marry a beautiful princess of good upbringing. One night, there was a storm. There was a knock on the door and the queen found a girl standing outside. She was wet and shivering. She said, "I am a princess but I got caught in this storm. Please may I stay here tonight?" The queen wanted to test if she really was a princess or not. So, while the servants made the bed, the queen placed a tiny pea on it and added many layers of mattresses and quilts on top. The princess slept on this bed.

The next day, the queen asked if she had slept well. She replied, "The bed was soft, but I could not sleep. I don't know what there was on it but my back has turned all blue!" Seeing how delicate she was, the queen realised that she was indeed a real princess of delicate upbringing. The prince was very pleased and married the princess and they lived happily ever after.

# 21 The Hen That Laid Golden Eggs

A poultry farmer found a stray hen and took it home. Lo and behold! The next day the hen had laid a golden egg! The farmer and his wife couldn't believe their luck. The farmer soon became very rich because the hen laid a golden egg every day. The foolish farmer then became greedy. One day, he thought, "If I kill this hen, I can take out all the golden eggs from its stomach together. Then I can sell all the eggs and become rich, even faster!" In the hope of finding lots of golden eggs within, he killed the hen. But of course he found no eggs. He was very upset and cried over his foolishness. Out of greed, he had robbed himself of even what he had. He had learnt his lesson but it was too late.

# 22 Three Jolly Fishermen

Three jolly fishermen went out to sea on a boat. They loved music. So, whenever they went out to fish, they would sing different songs depending on the mood of the sea. If the sea was calm, they would sing quiet lullabies but when the boat moved up and down they sang merry songs. When stormy winds blew over the sea and the waves crashed at the boat, they sang loud opera.

But the fishermen were never able to catch any fish. And do you want to know the reason why? Whenever the fishermen sang, they made such a noise that the fish would hear them and hide under their boat. So, the fishermen never caught any fish.

Soon, the fish too joined the three fishermen by singing along. All the fishes and lobsters and crabs were so busy singing and learning new songs that they never got caught. Thus, they were saved from landing on plates for dinner!

## 23 The Shoemaker and the Elves

Jo was a shoemaker who lived with his wife Margaret. They were very poor. One day, there was no more leather left. Jo had no more material to make shoes. Hungry and miserable, they went to bed.

When they woke up the next day, Jo and Margaret found a shining pair of beautiful shoes. They wondered where these shoes had come from. A man, who was passing by, saw the shining shoes and bought them at a good price. Jo was very happy. Margaret and Jo had a hearty meal that night. The next morning, when Jo went to his work shed, he saw another pair of new shiny shoes. He told his wife the good news. Margaret was surprised and happy but very puzzled. The two decided to keep a watch that night to find out who was being so kind to them.

In the middle of the night, when everybody else was asleep, Jo and Margaret waited secretly in the working shed. At midnight, they saw two elves! The elves were deep in their work, making shoes for them. By morning, they had made many new shoes. Jo and Margaret were filled with gratitude. When they saw the elves had nothing to wear they decided to make new, warm clothes for

them as winter was approaching. They kept their gift in the work shed the next night and hid behind the door. At midnight, the elves came again and saw the beautiful, tiny clothes. The elves were so happy with their new clothes that they sang and danced all night. They now knew that Jo the shoemaker and his wife no longer needed their help, and went away to help someone else in need.

## 24 The Nail

A tradesman had done a good day's business at a fair. The next morning, he took his bag of money and rode off on his horse planning to reach home by evening.

On the way, he stopped at an inn for lunch. A stable boy told him that a nail was missing in the shoe of the left foot of the horse. But the tradesman did not listen to him as he was in a hurry to reach home. A little later, the tradesman was advised by another stable boy

to fix a nail on the horse's shoe but yet again he didn't pay attention to him in his hurry to reach home as soon as possible. The horse began to limp after some time and soon it fell down and broke its leg. The tradesman had to leave his horse on the way and walk home. On the way, two robbers attacked him and stole his money.

As the tradesman walked home, battered and beaten, he regretted not fixing the nail on the horse's shoe in his haste to reach home.

## 25 The Conceited Apple Branch

It was spring. The apple tree was fresh and blooming. Soon a branch was cut off for a countess and put in a shining vase on a windowsill for all to admire. The branch became proud of its beauty. It began to despise the herbs and dandelions and called them ugly. With each passing day, the branch became more and more vain

But the wise sunbeam, which visited the windowsill every day, taught the apple bough that all creations are alike and beautiful in the eyes of God. God loves everyone equally, just as the sunbeam spreads its light on all in equal measure. The bough saw how the dandelions gave pleasure to the children as they came in the fields and plucked them to make a wreath.

A little later, the countess came in holding something very carefully. She placed a small dandelion flower along with the apple branch and said, "Both the branch and this humble flower are beautiful in their own way."

## 26 The Peasant in Heaven

A poor peasant arrived at the gates of heaven after his death. There, a very rich man was also standing, waiting to get into heaven, at the same time.

Saint Peter came with the key to heaven. He took the rich man inside but forgot to take the poor man. The poor man heard music and rejoicing inside for the rich man. The rich man was given lavish food and new clothes. The poor man expected to get the same welcome when it was his turn but neither was he given the same food nor new clothes. The angels took him in lovingly but no one sang for him. Seeing this, he asked Saint Peter why there was partiality in heaven.

Saint Peter replied that he was equally dear and would enjoy every heavenly delight like the others. But poor people like him came to heaven every day whereas rich men came rarely.

## 27 The Eagle, the Cat, and the Wild Sow

An eagle had made its nest at the top of an oak tree, a cat had made its home in a hole in the middle and a sow moved into a hollow at the bottom of the tree. The cunning cat did not want the eagle and the sow to live near her. So she thought of an idea to get rid of them.

She went to the eagle and told her that the sow was trying to uproot the tree so as to eat her young ones once the tree fell down. Then the clever cat went to the sow and said, "The eagle doesn't like you and has made a plan to attack your little ones and eat them. You must be careful, my friend." The sow thanked the cat for warning her of the eagle's intentions.

Both the eagle and the sow believed the cat and did not leave their homes in fear of each other. As a result, they along with their families, died of hunger and starvation and the wicked cat had enough and more food for herself and her kittens.

## 28 Odds and Ends

Once, there lived a maiden who was very pretty but lazy. Whenever she had to work, she was in a bad mood. She was very proud of her beauty. She had a hardworking maidservant who used to gather all the bits of flax the maiden threw away while spinning. With this, the maid spun a beautiful gown for herself. The lazy girl was about to get married to a young man. On the eve of her wedding, she saw her maidservant dancing in her new gown. The bride looked at her and said, "Look at her, dancing in the gown made from what I had thrown away." She told the groom about it.

The groom was impressed to hear how hardworking the poor girl was. He left the lazy girl and chose to marry the poor maid.

# Contents

*The Story of the Month:   Jack and the Beanstalk*

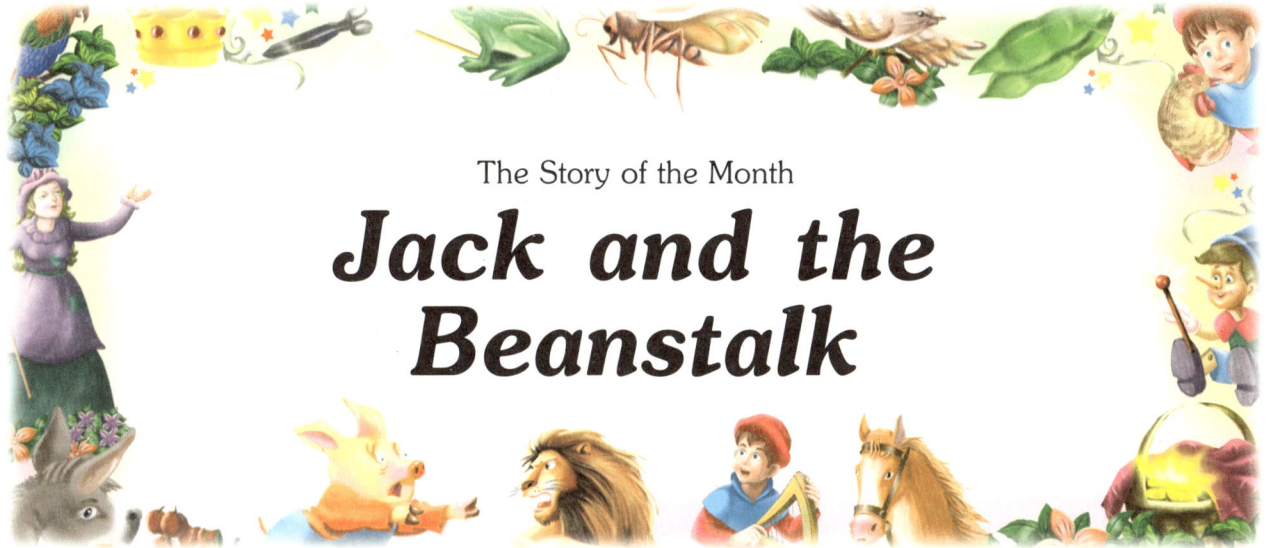

The Story of the Month

# Jack and the Beanstalk

## Jack and the Beanstalk

Once upon a time there lived a poor widow and her son Jack. One day, Jack's mother told him to sell their only cow. Jack went to the market and on the way he met a man who wanted to buy his cow. Jack asked, "What will you give me in return for my cow?" The man answered, "I will give you five magic beans!" Jack took the magic beans and gave the man the cow. But when he reached home, Jack's mother was very angry. She said, "You fool! He took away your cow and gave you some beans!" She threw the beans out of the window. Jack was very sad and went to sleep without dinner.

The next day, when Jack woke up in the morning and looked out of the window, he saw that a huge beanstalk had grown from his magic beans! He climbed up the beanstalk and reached a kingdom in the sky. There lived a giant and his wife. Jack went inside the house and found the giant's wife in the kitchen. Jack said, "Could you please give me something to eat? I am so hungry!" The kind wife gave him bread and some milk.

While he was eating, the giant came home. The giant was very big and looked very fearsome. Jack was terrified and went and hid inside. The giant cried, "Fee-fi-fo-fum, I smell the blood of an Englishman. Be he alive, or be he dead, I'll grind his bones to make my bread!" The wife said, "There is no boy in here!" So, the giant ate his food and then went to his room. He took out his sacks of gold coins, counted them and kept them aside. Then he went to sleep. In the night, Jack crept out of his hiding place, took one sack of gold coins and climbed down the beanstalk. At home, he gave the coins to his mother. His mother was very happy and they lived well for sometime.

A few days later, Jack

climbed the beanstalk and went to the giant's house again. Once again, Jack asked the giant's wife for food, but while he was eating the giant returned. Jack leapt up in fright and went and hid under the bed. The giant cried, "Fee-fi-fo-fum, I smell the blood of an Englishman. Be he alive, or be he dead, I'll grind his bones to make my bread!" The wife said, "There is no boy in here!" The giant ate his food and went to his room. There, he took out a hen. He shouted, "Lay!" and the hen laid a golden egg. When the giant fell asleep, Jack took the hen

and climbed down the beanstalk. Jack's mother was very happy with him.

After some days, Jack once again climbed the beanstalk and went to the giant's castle. For the third time, Jack met the giant's wife and asked for some food. Once again, the giant's wife gave him bread and milk. But while Jack was eating, the giant came home. "Fee-fi-fo-fum, I smell the blood of an Englishman. Be he alive, or be he dead, I'll grind his bones to make my bread!" cried the giant. "Don't be silly! There is no boy in here!" said his wife.

The giant had a magical harp that could play beautiful songs. While the giant slept, Jack took the harp and was about to leave. Suddenly, the magic harp cried, "Help master! A boy is stealing me!" The giant woke up and saw Jack with the harp. Furious, he ran after Jack. But Jack was too fast for him. He ran down the beanstalk and reached home. The giant followed him down. Jack quickly ran inside his house and fetched an axe. He began to chop the beanstalk. The giant fell and died.

Jack and his mother were now very rich and they lived happily ever after.

# 1 Simple Simon

A squire had three sons. The first two were very clever and knowledgeable. But the third one was called Simple Simon, as he did not know much and was very simple.

One day, the princess of a neighbouring kingdom announced that she would marry the person who could outwit her in speech.

The two clever sons decided to go and try to woo the princess over. Simon decided to go along with his brothers to give them company.

The squire gave his first two sons splendid horses for the journey while Simon rode a billy goat.

On the way, he found a crow, a clog (a cooker with a tin handle), and some fine mud, which he put into his knapsack. His brothers laughed heartily at this.

When they reached the princess's palace, the first two brothers, like so many others, became tongue-tied in the princess's presence.

But Simple Simon remarked "Oh! This place burns like a furnace." "I am roasting cockerels," said the princess.

"It is hot enough to roast a crow as well!" said Simple Simon.

The princess quickly replied, "Only if we had a pot or pan, for I have none."

"Well! Here's a clog," said Simon.

"What about the gravy to go with the dish?" asked the princess. "This fine mud will be just right," said Simon.

"I will marry you, for you are so witty," said the princess. So Simple Simon married the princess and became a prince.

# 2 The Nightingale

There lived an emperor in China, who had a very beautiful kingdom. Everyone admired his palace and gardens but when they heard the nightingale sing, they declared that it was the best of all. When the emperor heard about the nightingale, he sent his men to bring it for him. When he heard it sing, tears came to his eyes. He kept the bird in his palace in a cage.

One day, the king of Japan sent a beautiful artificial nightingale. This nightingale was covered with precious gems and sang wonderfully too. But it could sing only one song. Everyone forgot the real nightingale, and sadly it flew away. Then, one day, the artificial bird broke its spring and could not sing any longer.

Years passed. The emperor fell ill and was near death. No doctor could cure him. The real nightingale heard this and came to sing for him. Hearing it, the emperor recovered. The bird promised that it would always come and sing for him.

# 3 Forgetful Mr. Tinkle

Mr. Tinkle was a forgetful man. He would forget to open his umbrella when it rained. And then of course he would catch a cold. Mrs. Tinkle was worried about him. She decided to ask Witch Simple for help. She told her how Mr. Tinkle would never look up at the sky to see when it was going to rain. He would always walk with his eyes on the ground. Witch Simple suggested they put something on the ground to warn him of the rain. White flowers grew in the fields where Mr. Tinkle loved to walk. Witch Simple painted them bright red. Then she put a rain-spell on them so they would close up their petals whenever rain was near. The flowers were called Scarlet Pimpernel. Now when Mr. Tinkle saw these flowers close their petals he knew he had to put up his umbrella.

# 4 The Donkey Skin

Once there lived a pretty little girl named Rosalind. She lived with her cruel stepmother and her ugly daughter. The stepmother was jealous of Rosalind's beauty and always wanted her daughter to be prettier than Rosalind.

One day, the stepmother went to the market to buy warm clothes. She got her daughter a lovely fur coat and poor Rosalind a donkey skin. When Rosalind put it on, the donkey skin got stuck to her and would not come off!

Everybody made fun of her and heartbroken Rosalind ran away into the woods. She sat under a tree and sobbed her heart out. A prince chanced to pass by. When he saw Rosalind crying he began to play his magic lute. And lo! The donkey skin peeled off Rosalind's body!

The prince was captivated by Rosalind's beauty and fell in love with her. He took her to his kingdom and they were married and lived happily ever after.

## 5 The Troublesome Fly

Once upon a time there lived a bald farmer. One day, he was sitting in the verandah. A packet of sweets lay nearby. Some flies hovered over them. One of them left the tray and started buzzing around the farmer's head. The farmer bore it for a while. But the fly kept on irritating him and buzzing around his head.

The farmer finally grew impatient and struck his head with both hands. But the fly was quicker. It would escape each time the farmer tried to strike it. Finally the farmer realised he was only bruising his own head. He gave up trying to hit the fly.

He had learnt his lesson. We sometimes hurt ourselves by getting bothered about little things. It is better to ignore them.

## 6 The Clever Parrot

Once, there lived a merchant who had a beautiful daughter. Both the king and the viceroy loved her.

One day, the merchant decided to go away for a few days on business. When the viceroy heard that the merchant was leaving on business, he asked a witch to turn him into a parrot. Before leaving, the merchant bought the parrot for his daughter.

The viceroy knew that the king would woo the merchant's daughter as soon as the merchant left. In the form of the parrot he said to the girl, "I will tell you a story but while I'm telling it to you, you will not meet anyone." When the servant came to inform her there was a letter from the king, she refused to receive it in her father's absence.

When the merchant returned, the parrot disappeared. The viceroy asked the merchant for his daughter's hand and he agreed. The king died of a broken heart. The viceroy had been cleverer than him.

## 7 The Emperor's New Clothes

Once upon a time there was an emperor whose only interest in life was to dress up in fashionable clothes. He kept changing his clothes so that people could admire him.

Once, two thieves decided to teach him a lesson.

They told the emperor that they were very fine tailors and could sew a lovely new suit for him. It would be so light and fine that it would seem invisible. Only those who were stupid could not see it. The emperor was very excited and ordered the new tailors to begin their work.

One day, the king asked the prime minister to go and see how much work the two tailors had done. He saw the two men moving scissors in the air but he could see no cloth! He kept quiet for fear of being called stupid and ignorant. Instead, he praised the fabric and said it was marvellous.

Finally, the emperor's new dress was ready. He could see nothing but he too did not want to appear stupid. He admired the dress and thanked the tailors. He was asked to parade down the street for all to see the new clothes. The emperor paraded down the main street. The people could only see a naked emperor but no one admitted it for fear of being thought stupid.

They foolishly praised the invisible fabric and the colours. The emperor was very happy.

At last, a child cried out, "The emperor is naked!"

Soon everyone began to murmur the same thing and very soon all shouted, "The emperor is not wearing anything!"

The emperor realised the truth but preferred to believe that his people were stupid.

## 8 The Turquoise Fairy

One day on his way home, Pinocchio met a fox and a cat who wanted to steal his money. They told him that they would show him a meadow the next day where, if he planted his money, one gold coin would grow into a tree full of coins. They stayed at an inn overnight but when Pinocchio awoke in the morning he found them gone. He set off for home once again. Disguised as bandits, they caught him on the road and tied him up but a good fairy came to his rescue.

The Turquoise Fairy as she was known, took Pinocchio to her castle. When she asked him where the gold coins were Pinocchio lied and said he had lost them though they were in his pocket. To his horror his nose started growing longer. The fairy laughed and made his nose go back to its usual size.

"Now don't tell a lie again or it will grow long," she warned.

"I promise," said Pinocchio. He hugged the fairy gratefully and returned to Gepetto.

The next day, Betushka decided that she would not dance but would finish her spinning. But when she heard the maiden's voice, she could not stop herself from dancing. The fairy finished the spinning for Betushka. The next day when Betushka was returning home, the fairy told her not to look inside her bag till she reached home. But Betushka was very curious to see what was inside. She was very disappointed to see that there were only dry birch leaves inside. In anger, she threw away some of them.

When Betushka returned home and her mother saw the bag, she was surprised to see that there was gold inside. Betushka told her all about the fairy. Now their days of poverty were over. They bought a farm with a garden and cows and Betushka wore lovely dresses and no longer grazed goats.

# 9 The Wood Fairy

A cheerful little girl named Betushka lived with her poor mother in a small cottage. Every day, she took the goats to graze. Her mother would put an empty spindle in her bag and Betushka would spin while watching the goats. At midday, she would dance and sing merrily and in the evening she returned home with the spindle full of flaxen thread.

One spring day, when Betushka was about to dance, a beautiful maiden appeared suddenly in front of her. This maiden was the Wood Fairy. She asked Betushka to dance with her and both of them danced away till evening. Betushka forgot her spinning but when she reached home, she did not tell her mother about the lovely maiden.

# 10 The Dog and the Wolf

A hungry wolf was on the prowl. He met a dog passing by and requested him for some food. The dog took pity on the wolf and said, "Cousin, you should also work for a master like me. You will be given good food every day." The wolf agreed to go with the dog to his master's place so that he could share the dog's work. On the way, the wolf noticed that the hair on a certain part of the dog's neck was worn away.

He asked the dog how that happened. "Oh," the dog replied, "its just a little thing that's happened because of the collar that's put to chain me every night. Earlier it used to annoy me but now I'm used to it so it hardly matters." On hearing this the wolf said, "I think this is not the right place for me to work in, so I am leaving."

The wolf thought that it is better to be free and starve than to be a slave and eat well. He thought that he was better off than the dog and went away.

# 11 The Proud Frog

A large frog who was very vain believed that he was the most handsome frog and wanted to grow even bigger. He often admired his reflection in a pond and swelling with pride would boast to his friends, "Look how big I am!"

One day, an ox was passing by the pond. The proud frog looked at the ox and asked his friends, "Am I as big as the ox?" His friends, who were tired of hearing the proud frog boast about himself every day said that he wasn't as big as the ox.

The proud frog was furious and wanted to prove his friends wrong. He puffed himself up to become bigger and bigger to show his friends that he could be as big as the ox. He huffed and he puffed and all of a sudden, he burst and that was the end of the vain frog!

# 12 The Brilliant Idea

Once, a flock of doves were flying together in search of food. Soon, they saw some grains scattered on the ground below. They settled on the ground to pick the grains.

Unfortunately, a hunter had laid a net over the grains and they were trapped. They struggled hard to free themselves but could not. They heard the hunter approaching. Then the leader of the doves commanded them to flap their wings and fly together. Each dove picked up a part of the net in its beak and flapped its wings and lo! They were up in the sky.

The leader directed the doves towards a particular region. When they reached their destination and descended, the leader called out for his friend and from a hole nearby, out came a mouse. As soon as he saw the doves trapped, he quickly called all his friends and together, all the mice cut the net with their sharp teeth and set the doves free. The doves thanked the mice and flew away.

## 13 The Pixie Plumber

It was Midsummer Day, the day to meet fairy people. "I'd like to meet a pixie," said Jill to her brother Billy. "Mummy, will you help us?"

"I'm too busy," said Mummy. "I need a plumber, but Mr. Wrench is on holiday. I think I'll try Mr. P. Pixie."

Soon, a tubby little man in green overalls and a round green cap came knocking on the door. Jill and Billy watched him work with nimble fingers. Suddenly, his cap slipped and Jill and Billy saw his pointed ears.

"Why, you're a pixie!" exclaimed Jill.

"That's right," said Mr. Pixie. "And I'm here because you believed in me and for that there's some lemonade for you from the tap. Only for today of course," he added grinning.

Mummy was very happy with Pixie Plumber's work and wanted to call him again. But, alas, she never did find his number in the phone book again.

## 14 Rip Van Winkle

Rip Van Winkle was a lazy man. He would often go off into the forest with his dog, Wolf, to hunt for squirrels. One day, Rip helped a strange old man carry a barrel to a clearing where several others were playing a game. Rip had some of the pink water from the barrel along with his companions. Soon he fell sleep. When he awoke he was alone. Rip looked for his gun. To his surprise it was covered in rust! Feeling confused and hungry, Rip headed for his village. People gathered around him staring at his tattered clothes and long grey beard. Rip saw a young woman who looked like his wife and asked her who she was. She told him her name and said her father had left the house twenty years ago with his dog and never been seen again. "I am your father," cried Rip joyfully and told them all how he had been asleep for the last twenty years!

# 15 The Dancing Monkeys

A prince had monkeys in his court that could dance. As monkeys are natural mimics, they looked wonderful in their rich clothes and masks, dancing very much like human beings. Word spread far and wide about their unique performance and people from all over flocked to see them perform every day. Everyone was amazed at the monkeys' intelligence.

One day, a mischievous courtier thought of playing a trick on the monkeys. When the monkeys were dancing, he took a pocketful of nuts and threw them upon the stage. As soon as the monkeys saw the nuts, they forgot dancing and leapt to grab them. They pulled off their masks and tore their robes fighting with each other for the nuts. Everyone started laughing at the entertaining sight.

The people realised that even though they looked like humans they actually were animals.

# 16 The Three Little Pigs

Once upon a time there were three little pigs. One pig built a house of straw while the second pig built his house with sticks. They built their houses very quickly and then sang and danced all day because they were lazy. The third little pig worked hard all day and built his house with bricks.

A big bad wolf saw the two little pigs while they danced and played and thought, "What juicy tender meals they will make!" He chased the two pigs and they ran and hid in their houses. The big bad wolf went to the first house and huffed and puffed and blew the house down in minutes. The frightened little pig ran to the second pig's house that was made of sticks. The big bad wolf now came to this house and huffed and puffed and blew the house down in hardly any time. Now, the two little pigs were terrified and ran to the third pig's house that was made of bricks.

The big bad wolf tried to huff and puff and blow the house down, but he could not. He kept trying for hours but the house was very strong and the little pigs were safe inside. He tried to enter through the chimney but the third little pig boiled a big pot of water and kept it below the chimney. The wolf fell into it and died.

The two little pigs now felt sorry for having been so lazy. They too built their houses with bricks and lived happily ever after.

# 17 The King's Curse

A king had six sons but no daughter. He and his queen longed for a baby girl. When the queen was about to give birth to another child, the king declared that if this were a son too then all the children would be cursed.

Soon he had to leave for war. While leaving, he told the queen that she should hang a lance on the window if a son was born, and a distaff if a daughter was born. A girl was born but in the confusion and merrymaking, a lance was hung instead of a distaff. Seeing it on his return, the king cursed his sons. As a result they had to wander in the world unknown.

When the girl grew up she left to search for her brothers. She met an old man who told her that she would be able to find her brothers if she did not speak for seven years. Searching, she arrived at a king's palace. The king was struck by her beauty and married her. But she never spoke a word. The king's mother was unhappy with this marriage. When the queen was about to give birth to a child, she cunningly sent the king to war and imprisoned the queen inside a wall and sent a message to the king that his queen was dead.

But a servant rescued the queen and the child and took them to his house. He looked after them.

Seven years passed and the king returned. The queen could speak again and told the king the truth. The king rewarded the servant and helped the queen unite with her brothers. The brothers and sister went to meet their parents and lived happily ever after.

# 18 Old Mother Goose and Her Son Jack

A poor boy named Jack lived with his mother, old Mother Goose. One day, old Mother Goose sent Jack to the market to buy a fine goose. On the way, Jack rescued a beautiful young lady from a thief who was trying to steal her mantle. She happened to be the squire's daughter. Jack fell in love with her and would dream all day of marrying her.

One day, to his surprise, he saw that the goose he had bought, had laid a golden egg. Jack sold the egg at once in the market. Dressed in his finest clothes, he went to the squire's house to ask him for his daughter's hand. The squire was enraged and sent him back. But Jack was determined to win her. Every morning the goose laid a golden egg and soon Jack became a very rich man after selling the eggs. He became richer than the squire who at last, gave his consent and accepted Jack as his son-in-law.

## 19 The Fisherman and the Little Fish

A fisherman had been fishing all day and in the end all that he could catch was a small fish. He was disappointed but thought that at least he would have something to eat.

The little fish looked desolate and suddenly cried out, "Master, have pity on me and let me go. You can catch me again when I grow up and have a delicious meal. Right now I'm too small and my mother will be sad if you eat me. Please have mercy and let me off." But the fisherman replied, "Little fish, I've worked hard the whole day long and finally I've got you. I may not catch you later because by then somebody else may have already eaten you. How can I let you go?" So the moral of the story is that a little in hand is better than what is unknown in the future.

## 20 The Sparrow

A sparrow once ate all the grains put out by the woman next door. In a fit of anger, the ill-tempered neighbour cut the sparrow's tongue. Whimpering in pain, the poor bird flew away. Her mistress was heartbroken to find her beloved bird missing. She and her husband set out in its search. At last they found it perched on a tree in the nearby forest.

The sparrow welcomed them and laid out a special meal for them. When it was time to leave, the sparrow gave them a basket. On reaching home, they saw that the basket was full of gold and silver. From that day there was prosperity in their house.

Their neighbour was full of envy on seeing the change. She wished the same for herself and set out to find the sparrow. The sparrow gave her a basket too. But to her horror, she found that the basket contained not gold but frightful creatures that bit her. She realised her mistake and was ashamed of her deeds.

## 21 Fairy Dust

One morning the gnomes woke up to find their forest covered in a dreadful mist. Slowly the trees in the forest were beginning to die. "That wicked fairy, Meanice, has cast a spell!" said Gnome Midget. He was trying to figure out how to solve the problem. He first wanted to start clearing the forest of all the dead trees. So he took out his axe and set about chopping the trees. Now, the axe was a magical one handed down to him by his forefathers. As he chopped, pretty little fairies flew out of the tree stumps. And as they flew they strew fairy dust all over. Soon the whole forest was covered in fairy dust and it breathed fresh life into the trees. The forest was restored and all the magical creatures were happy to have their forest back again.

## 22 Peter Pan

One night Peter Pan took Wendy, John, and Michael to his home, Never Never Land. His fairy friend Tinker Bell dusted the children with fairy dust so they could fly.

The children were very happy playing there. Suddenly they found themselves surrounded by pirates! They huddled together in fear. "Put your hands by your side. March in a line!" ordered the captain.

All the children followed the captain as he led them to an old ship. Tinker Bell was passing through and saw them. She rushed to inform Peter Pan.

Peter and Tinker Bell found the children tied to the mast of the ship. They got ready to attack. "Beware! Here I come!" said Peter with a great cry as he jumped on the railing and challenged the captain to a fight. "Help me!" cried the old captain losing his balance and going overboard. "Hurrah!" the children and Tinker Bell cheered heartily for Peter Pan.

# 23 The Selfish Giant

A giant who lived in a big house had a beautiful garden, but he never let anyone enter his garden. Whenever he was away, children would come there to play.

One day, the giant decided to visit his friend and left for the neighbouring kingdom. The giant came back from his friend's place after seven years. Seeing the children play in his garden, he angrily chased them away and built a high wall around the garden.

After the children stopped coming to the garden, the trees and flowers were so sad that they lost their beauty and were covered with snow and frost. No birds came to sing there. Spring was everywhere but in the giant's garden it was still winter.

One morning, the giant saw children playing in the garden. They had entered through a small hole in the wall. And spring arrived in the garden at last to express its happiness on seeing the children again.

The giant realised that he had been selfish and was very sorry for what he had done. He let the children play in the garden every day. The giant's favourite among the children was a little boy who had kissed him when he helped him to get on top of the tree. But the little boy stopped coming to the garden and the giant was very sad.

Many years passed and the giant grew old and weak. One winter morning, the giant saw the same boy under a tree. He ran down to the boy in joy. The boy was an angel who had come to take the giant to the garden of Paradise as a reward for letting him play in his garden.

# 24 Lazy Jack

Jack was a simpleton who lived with his mother. One day, his mother told him to go out and earn money. They were very poor.

Jack went to work for a farmer and earned a penny. But while returning home, he dropped it in a brook. At home, his mother scolded him and told him to put his earnings in his pocket the next time.

The next day, he worked for a cow keeper, who gave him a jar of milk. Jack tried to put the jar of milk in his pocket and spilled it everywhere. Once again, his mother rebuked him. She told him that he should have carried it on his shoulders.

The next day, Jack was given a donkey. He carried the donkey on his shoulders. Now, the king had a daughter who never laughed. Seeing Jack carrying the donkey on his shoulders, she began laughing for the first time. As a reward, the king married her to Jack and they lived happily ever after.

## 25 A Feast Day

A boatman bought a fowl and told his wife to cook it for dinner. The wife put it to boil and then went for Mass.

In her absence, their cat and dog ate up the fowl. Then, scared of being taken to task for doing so, they tried to hide from their mistress. The cat jumped into the cobwebs near the beams and was stuck. The dog tried to get her out but he got stuck to the cat's tail.

Meanwhile, the mistress returned home. When she discovered that the cat and dog had eaten up the fowl, she was furious and wanted to give them a beating.

But while trying to pull them down, she got stuck to the dog's tail. Her husband tried to loosen the others but got stuck too. A friend who was passing by came to help them. He caught the husband from behind and pulled hard.

He pulled so hard that everyone came loose suddenly and fell higgledy-piggledy upon each other!

## 26 The Boastful Traveller

There was once a man who had travelled to many foreign places. On returning to his country, he boasted about his adventures and the heroic feats he had performed.

One day, while narrating his experiences to some bystanders he said, "When I was in Rhodes, I jumped such a great distance that no one else could beat me. I can call witnesses from Rhodes who saw me doing it." One person who had been listening to the man said that there was no need of witnesses. He asked the man to imagine he was in Rhodes and perform the same feat again.

At this, the man was taken aback as he had not expected this response.

He was trying to impress everyone and had not thought that anyone would challenge him. He quietly left the place and was never seen or heard boasting ever again.

## 27 The Doctor's Apprentice

A doctor took his apprentice to visit a patient. The apprentice was amazed that the doctor knew what his patient had eaten by just checking his pulse. When he asked the doctor the secret, he replied that doctors must never appear a fool in the patients' eyes. The doctor explained that he used to look under his patients' beds to check for crumbs and so would come to know what they had eaten.

The next day, the doctor sent the apprentice to visit the same patient. Trying to look like a skilful physician, the apprentice told the patient that he should not have eaten anything. The patient said that he had not even had a drop of water. The apprentice looked under the bed and confidently declared that he had eaten straw, as there were bits under his bed. The patient, who had heard the conversation between the doctor and the apprentice the day before replied, "Don't think I'm an ass like you are."

## 28 The Lion in a Farmyard

A lion entered a farmyard. As soon as he did, the farmer, who wanted to catch him, shut the gate. When the lion saw that he could not escape, he attacked the farmer's sheep and the oxen. Soon he had killed all the sheep and oxen and now the farmer feared for his own life. He opened the gate and let the lion escape.

The farmer was full of grief at the death of his sheep and oxen that had served him for many years. His wife had seen all that had happened. She was shocked to see her husband's stupidity and shouted at him and said, "How could you even think of shutting the lion inside when you start trembling at its mere roar?"

The farmer realised that sometimes it is harmful to be over courageous.

## 29 The Thoughtless Abbot

An abbot who was very wealthy only ate, drank, and slept the whole day. The priests became jealous of him and called him the "Thoughtless Abbot." They complained about him to the king. When the king asked the abbot, he replied that he slept the whole day because he had no worries and everything was taken care of by his servants.

The king decided to test him and gave him the impossible task of counting all the stars in the sky or else he would be beheaded. The abbot forgot to eat and drink in his fear. Finally, his old servant gave him an idea. When the king called for the abbot, the abbot ordered his servant to bring an ox hide. He told the king that there were as many stars as the number of hairs on the hide. And if he did not believe him he could have them counted.

The king was speechless at the abbot's answer and spared his life. The abbot thanked his servant and made him his steward.

## 30 The Gnat and the Lion

Once a gnat said to a lion, "I do not fear you at all. You are not stronger than me. All you know is how to show your claws and bare your teeth. I am much more powerful than you are. If you do not believe me then let us fight and see who wins. This will prove who is the stronger of the two."

Saying this, the gnat stung the lion on the nostrils and the other parts of his face.

The lion used his claws to swat the gnat and ended up hurting himself very badly.

Thus, the gnat was able to overpower the lion and feeling victorious, flew away.

Soon, he found himself stuck in a cobweb and was eaten by the spider. He could not believe what had happened to him.

He cried, "How is it possible that I, who defeated the mighty lion, should fall prey to this tiny insect!"

# 31 Ali Baba and the Forty Thieves

Ali Baba, a poor woodcutter was in the forest when he saw forty thieves stop in front of a cave.

The leader said "Open Sesame!" and before Ali Baba's amazed eyes the sealed mouth of the cave magically opened and the men disappeared inside. To come out and close the entrance, the leader said "Close Sesame" and the cave sealed itself once more. Trembling with excitement Ali Baba waited till the thieves had left and then entered the cave after saying the magic words. To his delight he found lots of treasure.

Ali Baba told his brother Kasim about the wondrous cave. Kasim set off to get some treasure for himself too. Sadly, he forgot the words to leave the cave and the thieves killed him. Ali Baba discovered his brother's body in the cave. With the help of a slave girl called Morgiana, he was able to take Kasim's body back home and bury it.

Realising that someone else knew about their cave the thieves tracked Ali Baba down. The leader, disguised as an oil seller stayed with Ali Baba. He had brought along mules loaded with forty oil jars containing the other thieves. Clever Morgiana knew who the oil seller really was and poured boiling oil into the jars killing the other thieves. While dancing in front of the leader of the thieves Morgiana stabbed him. Ali Baba was saved and lived happily ever after.

# Contents

*The Story of the Month: Rumpelstiltskin*

The Story of the Month

# Rumpelstiltskin

# Rumpelstiltskin

Once there was a poor miller who had a very beautiful daughter. One day, he went to the king's court and claimed that his daughter could spin straw into gold. The king ordered the miller's daughter to come to the palace. He took her to a room full of straw and said to her, "You must spin all this straw into gold tonight, or you shall die!" The miller's daughter was locked in the room alone. She did not know what to do and began to cry. Suddenly, a dwarf came out of nowhere and asked her, "Why are you crying?" When she

told him the story, he said, "Don't worry, I will spin the straw into gold, but what will you give me in return?" "I will give you my necklace!" she promised. The dwarf spun all the straw into gold.

The next day, when the king saw this, he was astonished and pleased. He became greedier. He took the girl to a bigger room and said, "Spin all this straw into gold or you shall die!" She was locked inside again, and once again she began to cry. The tiny man came into the room once more. He said, "If I spin all the straw into

gold, what will you give me this time?" She gave him her gold ring and he sat through the night and spun all the straw into gold.

The third morning, the king was very happy to see the room full of gold. He took her to the biggest room filled with straw and said, "If you spin all this straw into gold, you shall become my wife!" The girl was locked up and once again, she began to cry. This time, when the little man came to her, she said, "I do not have anything to give you, sir! What will I do?" He said, "Promise me that you will give me your first born child when

you become the queen!" The girl agreed to do so, because she was not expecting to become the king's wife. The tiny man spun all the straw into gold in the night. The next day, the king was pleased to see the gold. He married the girl and soon they had a baby.

The tiny man came to the queen to take her baby away but she had forgotten about the promise. She cried and begged him to leave her baby alone. The tiny man said, "I will not take your baby if you can guess my name! I will give you three days!" Saying this, he disappeared. The queen tried to remember all kinds of names. The next night, when

he came, she told him all the uncommon names she could think of, "Perhaps your name is Shortribs, or Sheepshanks, or Laceleg," but he always answered, "That is not my name." The next day the queen sent her servants all over the country to get all the possible names of the people. That night, the dwarf came to the queen again but she could not guess his real name.

On the third day, one of the queen's servants went into the forest to find the little man. Deep in the woods, the servant found him dancing and singing happily in front of

a fire. He sang, "Today I bake, tomorrow I brew, the next I'll have the young queen's child. Ha, glad am I that no one knew, that Rumpelstiltskin I am styled!" The servant went back to the palace and told the queen the name of the dwarf.

That night, when the little man came to the queen, she was already prepared. The tiny man challenged, "Do you give up? Shall I take your child away?" The queen smiled and replied, "Is your name Harry? Is it Conrad? Perhaps it is Rumpelstiltskin!" Hearing his name, the tiny man screamed, "How could you possibly know my name?" Saying this, he ran away, deep into the forest never to be seen again.

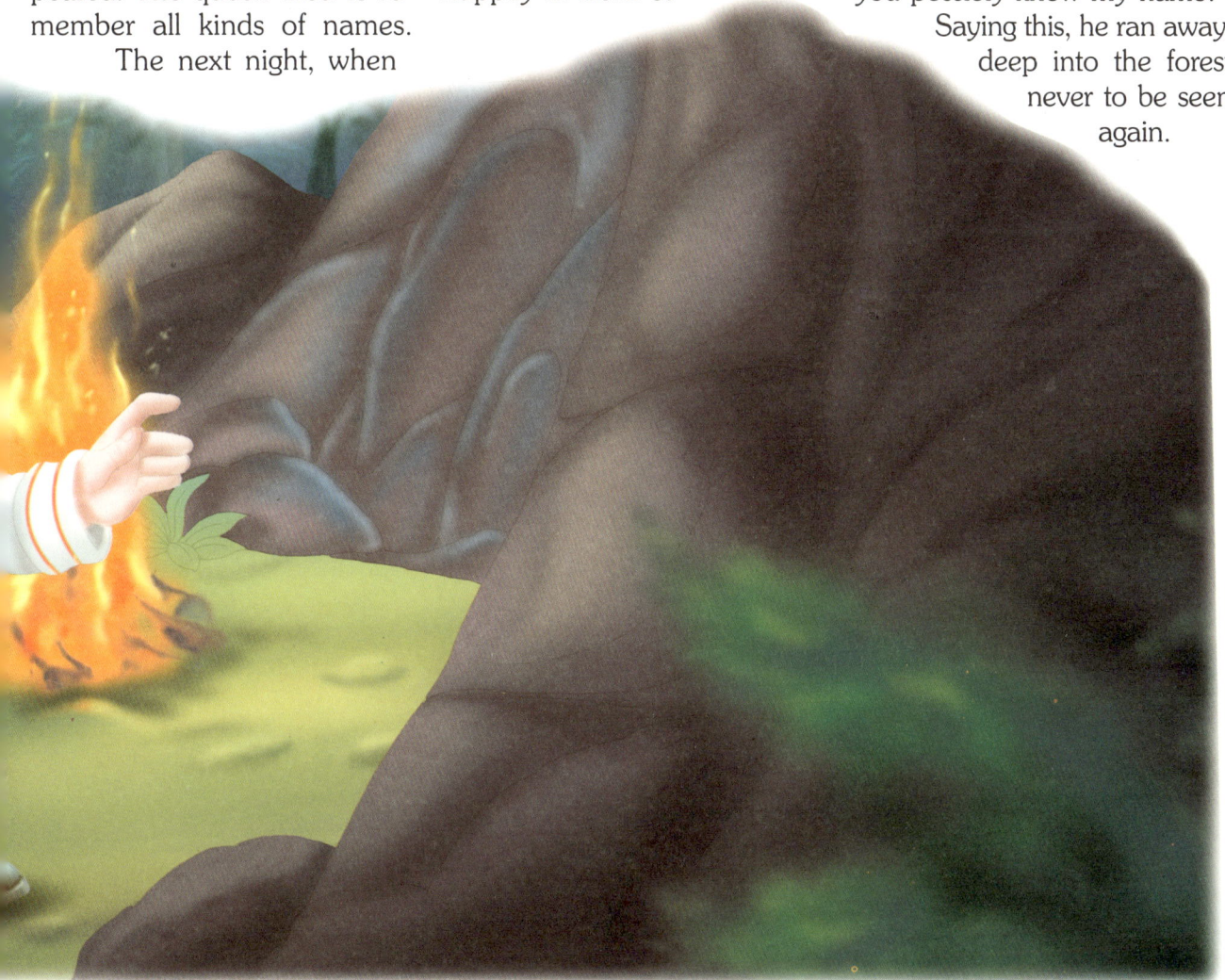

# 1 Buttercup

In the kingdom of Florin, there lived a maiden called Buttercup, who loved Westly. Westly was a farm boy who dreamt of becoming rich. One day, he sailed to America to fulfil his dream.

Buttercup missed him a lot and waited eagerly for him to return. One day, a man told her that the sea pirate Roberts had killed Westly. Buttercup was heartbroken.

Meanwhile, Humperdinck was the evil ruler of Florin. He wanted to make Buttercup his queen. However, he did not love her. His real aim was to kill her and put the blame on the ruler of the neighbouring country, so that he could wage a war against him.

Humperdinck hired Vizzini, and his two companions, Inigo Montoya and Fezzik to do the job. The three kidnapped Buttercup and fled Florin.

While escaping, they suddenly saw a masked man chasing them with a huge sword. He overpowered the three and whisked away Buttercup on his horse.

While struggling to free herself from the stranger, Buttercup tore open his mask. Before her stood Westly! He told her how Roberts had spared his life and set him free.

When Humperdinck learnt that Westly had found Buttercup, he sent his army to capture him. But Inigo, Montoya, and Fezzik took pity on the lovers and decided to help them. They joined forces with Westly and attacked Humperdinck.

After Humperdinck's death, Westly and Buttercup were married and lived happily forever.

# 2 The Musicians of Bremen

One day, Jack went out in the world to seek his fortune. On his way, he was joined by a cat, a dog, a goat, a bull, and a rooster. While camping in a house at night, they found a group of robbers inside. All of them screamed so hard that the robbers were scared and fled, leaving their loot behind. Jack knew that they would return to recover their money. He made the cat sit on a chair, the dog under the table, the goat on the stairs, the bull in the cellar, and the rooster on the rooftop.

Later, when the robbers returned they ran out of the house, screaming in fright. One robber spoke about an old lady sitting on the chair who had scratched him. The second robber complained about a shoemaker under the table who had hit him with an awl, while the third robber said that a man had knocked him down the stairs and hit him with an axe, and someone on the rooftop had also tried to hit him.

## 3 Flies and the Honey-Pot

When a jar of honey broke in a kitchen, some flies swarmed towards it and started eating the honey.

So absorbed were they eating honey that they did not even notice their wings and feet getting smeared with the sticky honey.

Having feasted to their heart's content, it was now time for them to leave. They tried to flap their wings, but they could not move. Then they tried to lift their feet but that too remained fixed.

Anxiously one fly cried, "Oh! Our greed has led us to our doom. We were so blinded by our hunger that we did not see the honey getting glued to our bodies."

Just then, a man entered to clean the kitchen. He took out a flyswatter and killed all of them.

## 4 The Clever Hare and the Lion

A lion who was the king of a jungle made a rule that every day one animal would be killed and its meat would be offered to him.

Accordingly, many animals had been sacrificed till one day it was the turn of a clever hare. He thought all night how he could save his life. Suddenly an idea struck him.

The next day, panting heavily, he reached the lion's den. He found the lion impatiently waiting for his dinner.

"Oh King, I am sorry to be late. There is another lion in a well who is threatening to capture your territory," huffed the hare. "Show me the villain! I will kill him!" roared the lion furiously.

The clever hare led him to a well filled with water. When the lion peered in, he saw his own reflection in the water. The foolish lion thought it to be the enemy and jumped into the well.

When the lion died the clever hare rejoiced and went back to tell all the animals that they had nothing to fear anymore.

## 5 Wicked and Kind

Once, there lived a farmer called Simon.

One winter evening, Simon was returning from his farm. On the way, he saw a snake lying still on the snow. Simon felt sorry for the snake and took him home. The snake wanted to be warm. He put the snake on the hearth, near the fire.

After some time, the snake started breathing and came back to life. Simon's son, Ben, was playing nearby. Seeing the snake moving he became curious and went to see what it was.

The snake raised its hood and was about to bite him, when Simon hit it with an axe and killed him. The farmer then realised that kindness may not always be repaid with kindness.

## 6 The Mad Hatter's Tea Party

Seven-year-old Alice was listening to her sister read a story under a tree when she saw a rabbit hurrying by. Curious to see where he was going in such a hurry Alice followed him. The rabbit scurried into a burrow and Alice followed him. Before she knew it she was falling down a long tunnel and found herself in a strange and wonderful place called Wonderland.

Wandering about she came across a tea party in progress. The March Hare and the Mad Hatter were sitting at one end of a long table with a dormouse between them. When they saw Alice they cried, "No room, no room!" "There's plenty of room!" said Alice firmly and sat down at the table.

The Mad Hatter and The March Hare were so rude and asked such stupid riddles and questions that Alice finally got fed up. "That was the stupidest tea party ever," thought Alice as she walked away in disgust.

## 7 Brother and Sister

A little brother and his little sister left their home because their wicked stepmother ill-treated them. On their way, the brother felt thirsty and went to a brook to drink water. But their wicked stepmother, who was a witch, had bewitched all the brooks. When the boy drank the water, he turned into a roebuck.

Meanwhile, the sister found a small house in the forest and the two started living there. Years passed and then one day, while the roebuck was wandering in search of food in the forest, the king and his huntsmen saw it. They tried to chase it but it safely returned home.

The king was very charmed by the roebuck and followed it to the cottage. He went up and knocked at the door. When the sister opened the door, the king was wonderstruck by her beauty. He immediately asked her to marry him. The girl agreed and went to live in the palace along with the roebuck, her brother. Soon a princess was born.

When this news reached the stepmother she became very jealous. She wanted her own daughter to become the queen. She killed the queen and made her daughter look like the young queen and put her in her place on her bed. The king did not know that this was a false queen.

Every night, the ghost of the true queen came to the room to feed her child and would stroke the roebuck's back. One night, the king stopped her, and she related the whole story to him. The angry king killed both the wicked witch and her daughter. Immediately, the queen regained life and the roebuck his human form again, and they lived happily ever after.

## 8 The Journey to the Moon

Once upon a time there lived an engine driver. He longed to go for a joy ride to the moon.

And one day, his wish was indeed fulfilled. His train got wings and he flew off to the moon. The driver saw the houses and trees getting smaller as the train soared higher and higher in the sky. "I am going to the moon!" he shouted with joy.

As the whistle blew and the train chugged on the moon, the people of the moon came out to catch a glimpse of this strange object. The driver stopped the train and asked them to board it. Surprised, they mounted the train and the wheels rolled again.

As the train zigzagged from one end of the moon to the other, the people on the moon jumped with joy and clapped their hands in glee.

Suddenly, the driver heard the sound of a bell. He woke up startled and realised that he had been sleeping and his journey to the moon had been just a beautiful dream.

## 9 The Fowler and the Viper

Once upon a time there was a fowler who lived in the village with his wife and two children. Once, on a bright and sunny day, he took his birdlime and twigs, and set out to catch some birds.

After walking for some time, he took out his pitcher and drank water. It was very hot so he sat under a tree and took a nap. When he woke up, he saw a thrush sitting on a tree in front of him. He watched the bird closely for some time and fitted his twigs to a proper length.

While he was thus looking, he did not realise that a viper lay sleeping before his feet. Suddenly, he felt a painful sting on his foot. The viper bit him and he began to swoon in pain. He sadly wondered, "I wanted to hunt a bird but it is my bad luck that someone else has trapped me to death."

## 10 Little Pigtails

Once upon a time, there lived a girl called Little Pigtails. She lived in the forest and played with all the animals. The animals adored her and she took care of them whenever they fell ill. One day, she saw a rabbit sobbing. He told her that a hunter had come to the forest and was shooting the animals. Little Pigtails was in tears. Then she saw the hunter aiming his gun at a bird and went up to him and said, "You must not shoot the animals! Don't you know it is a bad thing to do?" The hunter knew that she was right and was quite ashamed but hunting was his livelihood. Then Little Pigtails explained to him that he should not hurt these defenceless animals and he realised his mistake. He threw away his gun and became Little Pigtail's friend and never hurt the animals again.

## 11 The Cat and the Fox

A cat and a fox were good friends. One day, they argued about who was smarter. The fox boasted, "I know many tricks!" The cat knew only one. While they fought, they heard gunshots and the sound of hunters. The cat quickly climbed up a tree, while the fox tried many tricks. It danced and jumped but none of these tricks worked and the hunters soon caught him.

## 12 The Man, the Serpent, and the Fox

A hunter saved a serpent, which was almost crushed under a huge stone. On being released, the serpent said he was hungry and would eat the hunter. The man replied, "How can you be so ungrateful as to kill the person who saved your life?"

The serpent refused to listen to him. They decided to ask other animals to resolve this.

On the way, they met a grey-hound who said, "My master ill-treats me though I have served him for years. So the serpent is justified in eating the hunter." They met a horse who supported the serpent as well.

Finally, they met a fox. The fox thought awhile and asked the serpent to show him how and where he was buried. Thinking that he had already won the case, the excited serpent slipped into the hole. The fox then quickly lifted the stone and placed it on the serpent saving the hunter's life.

## 13 The Fox and the Woodcutter

Once a hunter was chasing a fox. The fox met a woodcutter and begged him to show him a hiding place and save his life.

The woodcutter showed him his hut. The fox crept in quickly and kept a watch outside. When the hunter came looking for the fox, the woodcutter pointed to the hut, but aloud he said he had not seen a fox. The hunter did not understand his signal and left.

Once the hunter was gone, the fox came out and was about to leave when the woodcutter said, "How ungrateful of you to leave without even thanking me for saving your life."

The fox turned back and replied sternly, "I would have thanked you provided your actions were as truthful as your words. You chose to help the hunter thinking that I would not see."

## 14 Truthful Joseph

Truthful Joseph never lied. One day, the king heard about Joseph and came to meet him. Impressed, the king placed him in charge of his cowshed.

Every morning, the king enquired about his animals, and Joseph replied, "Healthy and happy, Your Majesty." The king honoured Joseph before the noblemen of his court. The other servants grew jealous of Joseph's popularity and decided to lay a trap to trick him.

One day, a beautiful girl walked into Joseph's shed. Charmed by her he could refuse her nothing. He even killed a bull on her instructions. Once she left, Joseph realised his mistake. He grew worried and was scared that the king would punish him. As usual, the king called him the next day. Joseph told him the truth. The other servants had warned the king of Joseph's deed thinking he would be too frightened to tell the king the truth. The king was happy at Joseph's honesty and rewarded him.

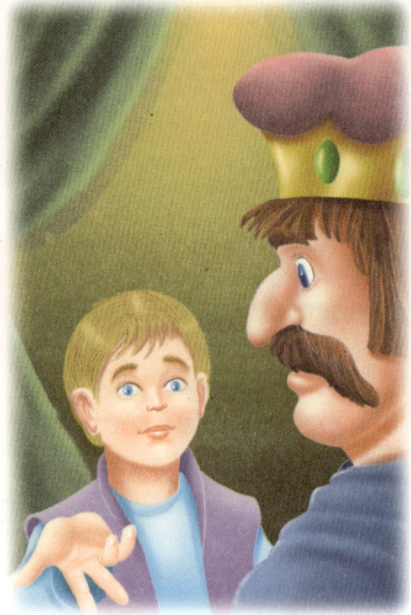

## 15 Why the Bear Is Stumpy-tailed

A bear saw a fox carrying a fish and asked the fox to teach him fishing. The fox decided to play a trick on the bear and replied, "Oh, its very simple. All you have to do is to dig a hole in the ice. Then put your tail into it and cover it with the ice. When it hurts, you will know that the fish has arrived and is nibbling your tail. Hold it for some time, then pull it sideways and you will get your fish."

The excited bear went to the icy river and did as the fox said. After sometime he felt his tail getting frozen. When it started aching, he remembered the fox's suggestion that the fish would bite it. Since the fox had asked him to wait for some time, he remained in that position for a while and then with great force, pulled it sideways. But to his dismay, his tail snapped off. That is why, bears are stumpy-tailed.

# 16 The Shepherd Boy

Once there was a shepherd boy who tended his sheep at the foot of a mountain. He used to feel lonely during the day. He thought of an idea whereby he could get some company and excitement. He went down to the village and shouted, "Wolf! Wolf." On hearing his shouts, the villagers came to save him. But no wolf was seen. The angry villagers went back.

The boy enjoyed this trick and after a few days repeated the same act. Once again the villagers came to help him. They realised they had been fooled once more by the naughty boy.

One day a wolf actually came to attack the boy and this time the boy shouted even louder than before. But the villagers thought that the boy was trying to fool them once again. So no one came out to help him and the wolf took the boy away.

As the wise saying goes, "No one can know when a liar speaks the truth."

# 17 Thumbelina

A kind woman who had no children, longed for a baby and would often say, "How I would love to have a baby girl, even a tiny little one."

A beautiful fairy heard her wish one day, and gave her a little seed to plant in a flowerpot.

When the seed bloomed into a tulip, the woman saw a tiny, beautiful girl inside, no bigger than her thumb. She decided to call her Thumbelina. She was so small that she had a walnut shell for a bed and used petals as a blanket.

Then, an ugly toad fell in love with Thumbelina. One night when she was sleeping, he carried her off to his lily pad in a pond. Thumbelina was very unhappy. A swallow was passing by and saw how sad she looked, and said, "Come south with me to warmer lands."

Young Thumbelina flew away on the swallow's back. They flew across the seas and came to a land of sunshine. The swallow said, " This is my home. You can live in one of the loveliest and biggest flowers." When Thumbelina stepped inside, she found a handsome fairy, as tiny as her, in its heart.

He was the son of the king of flowers and he fell in love with Thumbelina. He asked her to marry him. So Thumbelina became queen of the flowers and the two lived happily ever after.

## 18 Princesses of Whiteland

One day, while he was fishing, a fisherman saw a head pop out of the river and say, "You can catch plenty of fish if you give me the first thing your wife shows you when you go home."

When the fisherman went home, his wife showed him their newborn son. The man ran to the king for help. The king took the child under his care.

When the child grew up, he went fishing one day. While fishing, the waves carried him to an unknown land called Whiteland. There, he found three princesses planted inside the earth with only their heads sticking out. They told him how three wicked ghosts had captured their castle and planted them. He killed the ghosts and freed the princesses.

He married the youngest princess and began living there. But soon he wanted to visit his parents. The princess handed him a ring, which would fulfil any two wishes but warned him not to listen to his mother. He wished to reach home, and in a second found himself there.

On his mother's suggestion, he went to meet the king. The princess appeared, sorrowfully reminding him of her warning and then she disappeared.

The heartbroken boy began searching for her. He met a magician who gave him a pair of magic shoes that could fly him to Whiteland. While flying, the North Wind told him that another king wanted to marry the princess. With the wind's help he blew away the king and reunited with the princess.

## 19 Snow White and Rose Red

Once upon a time there lived two sisters, Snow White and Rose Red. One winter's day, they opened the door to find a shivering bear! They were frightened, but then feeling sorry for the bear, they let him in. The bear and the sisters became good friends. One day, after the bear had gone, they saw a dwarf in the forest. His beard was caught in a fish's mouth. Snow White saved him by snipping his beard off. This made the dwarf angry!

Another day, the dwarf's beard was stuck in a tree trunk and Rose Red snipped off his beard. Again he became very angry! One day, Snow White and Rose Red saw the dwarf hiding a treasure. When he saw them, he ran to beat them with a stick. The bear who saw all this, came charging at him. The dwarf died out of fright. Suddenly, the bear turned into a handsome prince! He had actually been bewitched by the dwarf. He married Snow White and his brother married Rose Red.

# 20 The Gamecocks and the Partridge

A man had two gamecocks on his farm. One day, he came across a partridge that was up for sale. He bought it and kept it along with his gamecocks. But the mischievous gamecocks did not let him rest in peace. They would follow the partridge and peck it just to trouble it. The partridge thought that just because he was a stranger he was treated badly. After some days, the partridge was surprised to see the two gamecocks fighting with each other until one of them was badly beaten by the other. From that day he thought, "I will no longer feel miserable when these gamecocks trouble me because when they keep on beating and quarrelling with each other then who can stop them from fighting with me?"

# 21 The Jinn in the Bottle

There was a jinn who could change his shape and cast spells on people. But one day the jinn misbehaved, so his master put him in a bottle and threw him into the sea. A passing fisherman had cast his net and when he pulled it in he saw the bottle. Feeling sorry for the jinn, the fisherman let it out.

Immediately the jinn became as big as a mountain and threatened to kill the fisherman. The fisherman pretended to be puzzled and said, "I know you can make yourself big but I doubt whether you can make yourself tiny." "Of course I can," roared the genie. "So small that you can get into this bottle?" asked the fisherman. The genie immediately shrank to the size of a fly. "But I doubt you could get into that bottle," scoffed the fisherman. No sooner had he said that then the genie entered the bottle and the fisherman plugged the bottle shut and tossed it the sea.

## 22 The Fox and the Mosquitoes

Once a fox was crossing a river on a bright, sunny day. After coming out of the river, he walked towards the forest. On his way, his tail got entangled in a bush and he was stuck. He could no longer move. Seeing the fox's condition, some mosquitoes sat on his tail and began to bite it and suck blood.

In the meantime, a hedgehog was passing by. He saw the fox in pain and took pity on him. He offered to help the fox by killing the mosquitoes or driving them away. But strangely, the fox refused the help. He said, "The mosquitoes are already full with my blood and cannot have more. If they are driven away fresh mosquitoes will come and attack me, and bleed me to death!"

## 23 Tattercoats

Once there lived an old man who disliked his granddaughter, because his own daughter had died while giving birth to her. The girl was given scraps of food to eat, a dilapidated bed to sleep on, and tattered clothes to wear. People called her "Tattercoats." Her only friend was a cowherd.

One day, her grandfather was invited to a ball at the king's palace. Tattercoats was sad that she couldn't go, so she decided to go visit her friend.

On her way, she met a handsomely dressed man carrying a magic flute. He asked Tattercoats to attend the ball at midnight. When Tattercoats arrived at the ball, everybody poked fun at her. But the handsome man started playing a wonderful tune on his pipe. Suddenly, Tattercoats' rags changed into a gorgeous dress with pretty jewels. The man then told the king, "Father, I want to marry this young maiden." Tattercoats was surprised to know that he was the prince and agreed to marry him.

# 24 The Pied Piper

The town of Hamlyn was once full of rats. They ate all the food, troubled sleeping babies, and made a lot of noise. The people had grown tired of the rats but were unable to do anything. Even the cats were not able to kill the rats.

One day, a queer fellow with piercing eyes, came to town. He was called the Pied Piper. He went to the Mayor and asked him, "What will you pay me if I free your town of every single rat?" The mayor offered fifty pounds to the Pied Piper.

Happy with the offer, the Pied Piper started playing his pipe. Hearing the shrill, keen note, every rat came out from its hole and started following him. The Pied Piper kept on playing his pipe and the rats followed him. The piper walked up to the harbour with millions of rats behind him and led them into the water and waited till every rat had drowned.

Now the town was free of the little devils and the people were very happy.

After all the rats were dead, the Pied Piper returned and asked the Mayor for his money. The Mayor said that he could only give him twenty pounds for such an easy job. Now that the rats were dead, the Mayor thought that there was nothing to worry about. But the Pied Piper wanted to teach him a lesson. This time he played a different tune. Hearing his music, the children came out of their houses. They started following the piper, dancing and shouting. The elders watched in disbelief as the Pied Piper led the children far, far away. The Mayor sent his men to look for the piper and bring the children back but none could find the lost children.

# 25 Sun, Moon, and Wind Go Out to Dine

One day, Sun, Moon, and Wind went out to dine with their uncle and aunt, Thunder and Lightning. Their mother, a distant star, waited for their return. Both Sun and Wind were greedy and selfish. They enjoyed the meal but brought back nothing for their mother. But the gentle Moon removed a portion of food and kept it under her beautiful, long fingernails to share it with her mother.

When they returned home, their mother asked them what they had got for her. Sun and Wind promptly replied that they had got nothing since they had gone for their own enjoyment. But Moon gave her mother the delicious food that she had brought for her.

The mother was angry with Sun and Wind for their selfishness and cursed them. That's why the sun is hated in hot weather and the wind is so disagreeable but the moon was blessed with good wishes. That is why she is always beautiful and cool.

## 26 Gertrude's Bird

One day, tired after travelling a great distance, Jesus decided to take rest. He entered a house owned by a woman named Gertrude. She had a red tuft of hair on her head.

Jesus asked her for some food and water. Gertrude wasn't too happy serving food to strangers at such an odd hour. Grudgingly, she took some dough to bake him a cake, but as she spread it on the table, the dough increased in size. Surprised, she took an even smaller piece, but it expanded too. This happened several times. Finally, she grew tired and told Jesus that she couldn't serve him anything.

Jesus cursed her to become a woodpecker. The bird flew up the chimney and turned black while passing through the smoke.

That is why woodpeckers have a red patch on their head and are black in colour.

## 27 Four Oxen and the Lion

In the forests, there lived four oxen. They were very good friends and always went together to graze in the fields. However, every time they went, a hungry lion tried to attack them. The lion longed for their meat. But they withstood his attack by fighting him as a team. They attacked him with their horns and the lion fled to another forest. One day, the four oxen fought among themselves. They started going to the forest separately. When the lion returned, he saw that the group was divided. He planned to take advantage of this situation.

Finding the first ox grazing in the fields alone, he crept from behind and ate him up. The next day, he attacked the second ox and killed it too. This way he killed the third and the fourth ox too. Had the four oxen stayed together, they wouldn't have lost their lives.

## 28 Sour Grapes

A hungry fox passed by a vineyard that was full of sweet grapes. When the fox saw the grapes, his mouth began to water. The fox tried to eat the grapes by jumping higher and higher. But the grapes still could not be reached. He finally gave up and walked away from the vineyard. Some birds perched on a tree nearby asked, "How are the grapes?" The fox complained, "The grapes are sour."

# 29 The Kid and the Wolf

Once, a kid was returning alone from the pasture. On the way, he saw a wolf chasing him. The poor kid was scared to death. He started running but the wolf kept following him. The kid realised that there was no way he could escape from the wolf and said to him, "My friend, I know I have to be your prey since I cannot escape from you. But before dying I want to ask you to fulfil a wish of mine. Can you sing me a tune so that I can dance?"

The wolf agreed and while he was singing, some hounds heard him and gathered near the wolf. They began to chase him. The wolf realised his mistake and said, "I should not have listened to you because my work is to kill and not sing tunes."

Thus, by quick thinking, the kid was able to save himself.

# 30 The Naughty Little Girl

Once upon a time there was a very naughty girl. She wanted to become a witch and cast a spell on all things around her.

So she began reading about witchcraft and went to the market nearby to buy a cauldron, a cloak, and a broomstick.

One night, she wore the cloak and prepared some magic potion in the cauldron. Then she swung her broomstick and in a minute everything in that room started to dance. The bed, the teapot, the plates, and the chairs—all shook vigorously and began banging against the girl and making a terrible noise. Frightened by these strange happenings, she ran out of the house, but they chased her. She finally managed to hide in a cave.

The girl understood her mistake. She realised that one should not do to others what one would not like to have done to oneself.

# Contents

The Story of the Month: Snow White

The Story of the Month

# Snow White

# Snow White

Once upon a time there lived a lovely princess with fair skin and blue eyes. She was so fair that she was named Snow White. Her mother died when Snow White was a baby and her father married again. This queen was very pretty but she was also very cruel. The wicked stepmother wanted to be the most beautiful lady in the kingdom and she would often ask her magic mirror, "Mirror! Mirror on the wall! Who is the fairest of them all?" And the magic mirror would say, "You are, Your Majesty!" But one day, the mirror replied, "Snow White is the fairest of them all!" The wicked queen was very angry and jealous of Snow White. She ordered her huntsman to take Snow White to the forest and kill her. "I want you to bring back her heart," she ordered. But when the huntsman reached the forest with Snow White, he took pity on her and set her free. He killed a deer and took its heart to the wicked queen and told her that he had killed Snow White. Snow White wandered in the forest all night, crying.

When it was daylight, she came to a tiny cottage and went inside. There was nobody there, but she found seven plates on the table and seven tiny beds in the bedroom. She cooked a wonderful meal and cleaned the house and tired, finally slept on one of the tiny beds. At night, the seven dwarfs who lived in the cottage came home and found Snow White sleeping. When she woke up and told them her story, the seven dwarfs asked her to stay with them. When the dwarfs were away, Snow White would make delicious meals for them. The dwarfs loved her and cared for her. Every morning, when they left the house, they instructed her never to open the door to strangers.

Meanwhile, in the palace, the wicked queen

asked, "Mirror! Mirror on the wall! Who is the fairest of them all?" The mirror replied, "Snow White is the fairest of them all! She lives with the seven dwarfs in the woods!" The wicked stepmother was furious. She was actually a witch and knew how to make magic potions. She now made a poisonous potion and dipped a shiny red apple into it. Then she disguised herself as an old peasant woman and went to the woods with the apple. She knocked on the cottage door and said, "Pretty little child! Let me in! Look what I have for you!" Snow White said, "I

am so sorry, old lady, I cannot let you in! The seven dwarfs have told me not to talk to strangers!" But then, Snow White saw the shiny red apple, and opened the door. The wicked witch offered her the apple and when she took a bite poor Snow White fell into a deep sleep. The wicked stepmother went back to the palace and asked the mirror, "Mirror! Mirror on the wall! Who is the fairest of them all?" The mirror replied, "You are, Your Majesty!" and she was very happy.

When the seven dwarfs came

home to find Snow White lying on the floor, they were very upset. They cried all night and then built a glass coffin for Snow White. They kept the coffin in front of the cottage. One day, Prince Charming was going past the cottage and he saw Snow White lying in the coffin. He said to the dwarfs, "My! My! She is so beautiful! I would like to kiss her!" And he did. Immediately, Snow White opened her eyes. She was alive again! The Prince and the seven dwarfs were very happy. Prince Charming married Snow White and took her to his palace and lived happily ever after.

# 1 Sindbad and the Roc

Sindbad was a merchant's son who travelled to many distant lands buying and selling goods. On one of the many voyages, the merchant ship stopped at a beautiful, tree-covered island where Sindbad decided to take a nap.

When he awoke he discovered that the ship had set sail without him! Looking for a way to get off the island he saw a large white dome. Just then a huge shadow fell over him. Looking up Sindbad saw a huge bird, called a Roc, and he realised that the white dome was actually the bird's egg. A brilliant idea came to him. "Let me tie myself to this bird's legs!" he thought. "Then, I can leave this island."

At daybreak when the Roc flew away over the sea, it carried Sindbad too. When it touched down Sindbad un-tied himself quickly before the Roc flew off again. He found himself in a valley full of diamonds, surrounded by steep mountains. Large serpents hid from the Roc in caves during the day and came out at night.

"Thud! Thud!!" Sindbad saw big chunks of meat landing on the valley floor. Merchants who wanted the diamonds were throwing them down from the ridges. They waited for the eagles to pick up the chunks of meat with the diamonds stuck on them, and take them to their nests from where the merchants would get the diamonds. Sindbad tied a piece of meat to himself. An eagle picked him up and carried him to its nest and in this way Sindbad escaped from the Valley of Diamonds.

# 2 The Silkworm and the Spider

Princess Lioness ordered the silkworm to spin twenty yards of silk for her royal robe. The silkworm sat by her loom and began the work eagerly.

One day, a spider came along and asked the silkworm if it could hire a web-room close by. The silkworm consented and the spider started to weave his web. He finished his work quickly and said to the silkworm, "See how delicate and lovely my web looks. And I have finished my work so quickly while you are so slow. Don't you agree that I'm a better worker than you?"

The silkworm replied scornfully, "Go away, you disturb me." Then she looked at the exquisite web she was making and said to the spider, "Your web is only a dirty trap for others and it can be easily destroyed, whereas what I design is beautiful and stored as a royal ornament."

Thus true art is something, which takes time to produce, lasts longer, and pleases all.

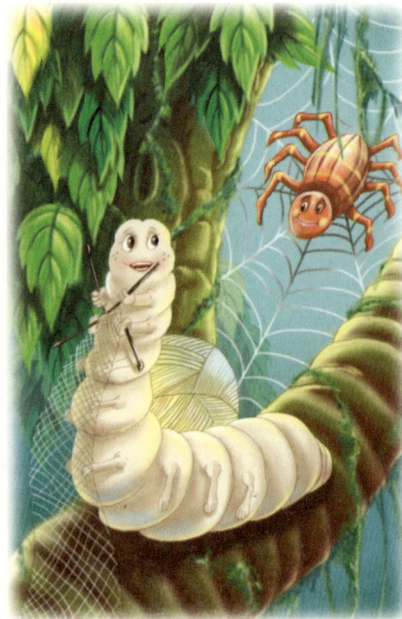

# 3 The Kites and the Swans

In olden times, kites and swans were blessed with an amazing talent. They could sing very well and used to entertain everyone, young and old, with their melodious voice. Sometimes they would even sing in the king's court. People came from far and wide to hear them sing.

One day, they heard the neigh of a horse. They were delighted by this unfamiliar sound. They thought the horse's neigh was better than their voice and wished that they could also neigh like the horse. So, they tried very hard to imitate that sound. As a result they forgot what they knew best—to sing. No one came to hear them anymore and praise their beautiful songs. In the desire to learn something that was not fit for them, they lost what they already had.

# 4 The Mouse and the Sun

A small boy, who lived on the snow-covered hills, came down to the plains to spend a day.

It was very hot in the plains and the feather coat that he was wearing shrank due to the heat of the sun. Not used to the heat, the boy was very angry and decided to punish the sun. He went back home and asked his sister to make a net with her hair.

The next morning he went to the top of the hill and just as the sun came up, he caught it in the net. That day the sun did not rise and the animals could not go out to look for food. They saw that the sun was trapped in a net and sent the mouse, which used to be very big in size at that time, to cut the net.

The mouse cut the net with his sharp teeth and freed the sun. All the animals were happy now and rejoiced. But due to the heat of the sun, the mouse had shrunk and become very small. That is why a mouse is so small in size.

## 5 Gulliver in Lilliput

After a fierce storm had wrecked his ship *Adventure*, Gulliver was washed ashore on an island called Lilliput. He awoke to a strange feeling all over his body. He found he couldn't move. He looked down and saw hundreds of tiny beings, less than six inches tall, swarming all over his body. The tiny Lilliputians had tied him to the ground so that he could not harm them. "I won't harm you," said Gulliver but the Lilliputians would not set him free. Gulliver promised to help them fight a neighbouring country called Blefuscu. Gulliver captured the enemy's navy with ease and helped the Lilliputians win the war. He became their hero and they made him part of the king's court. But because he longed to see his family, the Lilliputians agreed to let him go at last.

## 6 The Lamp

An old street lamp had shone and given light for twenty-four years. But this was his last day of work. He was to retire today. Next day, he would be taken in front of the mayor who would decide his fate. He would either serve in a village or in a factory or would be melted down in an iron foundry.

He remembered all the things he had seen from the post. He would certainly miss the watchman who had joined duty the night he was put up on the post. The watchman's wife would clean him and give him oil every day. With all these happy thoughts and memories, he sighed and went off to sleep.

To his surprise, the next night he found himself burning in the watchman's house. The watchman had begged the mayor to allow him to keep the lamp.

The old lamp was very happy for he could now live with the watchman's family forever.

# 7 The Little Golden Fish

Once there lived a poor fisherman and his nagging wife. One day, the fisherman went to the sea and caught a golden fish. The fish pleaded, "Oh, please let me go! I am the king of the sea! I will grant you any wish!" The fisherman was surprised to see the golden fish, and let it go. He went home and told this to his wife and she became angry. She said, "You fool! You should have asked for a new bathtub! Haven't you seen how bad our old one is?" So, the fisherman went to the sea again and told the golden fish about his wife's wish. When he came home, he found a brand new bathtub, but the greedy wife was not happy. She ordered, "Go to the fish again and ask him for a big house now!"

The fisherman was scared of his wife and he went to see the golden fish again. When the fish heard about the new wish he said, "I will grant you the wish because you are kind. Go, be happy!"

When the fisherman reached home, he found the wife in a palace wearing expensive clothes. But the ungrateful wife was still not satisfied and ordered, "Go find that fish right now and ask him to make me the queen of this world! Go!"

The witless fisherman ran to find the fish. However, this time, the little golden fish did not appear. Suddenly, there was a flash of lightning and a bolt of thunder. He ran home to find that the golden fish had taken back all the wishes. The fisherman realised that if he had not listened to his greedy wife, they would not have lost the bathtub or the palace and would have been very rich.

# 8 Stupid Catherine

Once upon a time there lived a girl named Catherine who was very stupid.

One day, she put some cakes in a basket to sell in the market. On the way, one of the cakes fell from her basket and rolled down the hill. Catherine thought, "Why should I bother going after it? I will send another cake to bring it back." So she rolled down another cake. When the cakes didn't return she rolled down a third cake to look for them. One by one, she rolled down all the cakes she had. Now her basket was empty. Catherine was annoyed and said, "If these cakes think I am going to waste time looking for them, they are wrong. I will go to the market alone and they will come on their own." When Catherine reached the market, her husband was very angry to see the empty basket. Catherine said, "Don't be angry, the cakes will come very soon." The husband realised how foolish his wife was and cursed his luck.

# 9 Rinkrank

Once upon a time there was a king who had a very beautiful daughter. She loved a young man. But the king did not approve of the match and said that he would allow him to marry the princess only if the young man could cross a glass mountain without falling. The princess decided to go with him too so that whenever he would start to fall she could hold him. The two started climbing the mountain. Unfortunately, the princess fell down and the mountain opened and swallowed her.

The princess had fallen into a cave deep inside the earth. An old man named Rinkrank made her his servant.

Every day, Rinkrank went up to the surface of the earth and he would return at night. He would hide the ladder he used so that the princess could not escape.

One day, when Rinkrank returned the princess refused to open the door. Rinkrank tried to enter through the window but the princess shut it and his beard got stuck.

He howled in pain and begged her to open it. The princess agreed on the condition that he should tell her where the ladder was. Rinkrank had no choice but to tell her. The princess tied one end of a rope to the window and with the other in her hand she climbed to the surface of the earth using the ladder. Climbing out, she pulled the rope and freed Rinkrank.

The king was very happy to see his daughter safe and happily married her to the man she loved.

# 10 The Lion and the Dolphin

A lion saw a dolphin playing in the sea. Seeing it frolicking among the mighty waves, he was impressed by the dolphin's power. He called out, "Let us be friends since I'm the king of beasts on the land while you are the ruler of the sea creatures." The dolphin happily agreed and they became good friends.

One day a wild bull attacked the lion. They fight continued for a long time as the bull was very strong. The lion was tiring and called out to the dolphin for help but the dolphin was unable to help.

The lion eventually defeated the bull. He went to the dolphin and said, "What kind of friend are you? I needed help and you did not bother to come." The dolphin explained to the lion, "Nature has made me powerful in the sea but I am helpless on land. You are so powerful but will be able to save me from danger in the sea?" The lion realised his mistake and the two remained friends.

# 11 Face-Off

A fox entered a dark room in a theatre. A face stared at him from the wall in front. "Aaah!" he jumped with fright and backed away. Finally, he mustered up a little courage and went to look more closely and found that the face was made of cardboard.

He saw many such faces lying around and realised that he was in one of the changing rooms. He thought, "These faces are used by the performers for their roles! Why am I getting so scared of these masks? They are not real and cannot harm me in any way."

Then the fox realised that if you look closely at your problems they will be nothing to worry about. Problems disappear when you are determined and are ready to face them and find a solution.

# 12 The Lonely Lion

While roaming the forest, a lion met a woodcutter and his lovely daughter. The lion demanded that the woodcutter give his daughter in marriage to him or he would kill him. The woodcutter was unwilling to agree to the lion's wish but he was afraid of refusing him and losing his life. He thought of a plan to rid himself of the lion.

The woodcutter told the lion he was ready to accept him as his son-in-law but had one condition. The woodcutter told the lion he would pull out his teeth and cut his claws so that his daughter would not be afraid of her husband. The foolish lion consented to the woodcutter's suggestion. Now the lion was toothless and didn't have any claws either.

When he expressed his wish to marry the beautiful daughter, the woodcutter was no longer frightened of the lion. He took his club and drove away the lion into the forest and found a suitable match for his daughter.

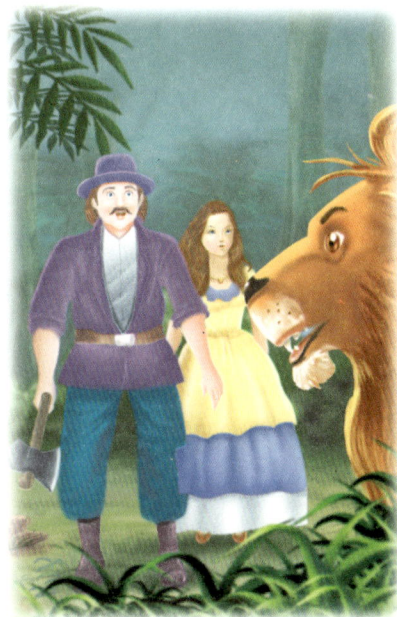

## 13 The Lion and the Boar

On a hot summer afternoon, a lion and a boar felt very thirsty. While looking for water to quench their thirst, they came to a well to drink water, but reached there at the same time. They quarrelled as to who would drink water first. Soon the quarrel turned into a violent fight and they started hurting each other.

The fight continued for a long time. Both of them were badly wounded but they continued fighting. At one point, they stopped to catch their breath and saw two hungry vultures sitting above them on a tree.

The vultures were looking at them and were waiting for them to kill each other, so that they could come down and feed on their bodies. This sight made the lion and the boar realise the uselessness of their fight.

They at once made up saying, "It is wiser for us to become friends rather than be eaten up by vultures and crows."

## 14 The Nightingale's Advice

One summer night, a man lay listening to a nightingale's song. He was so fascinated by the song that he captured the nightingale. He held it in his hands and said to it with pride, "Now you shall sing to me every night." But the nightingale replied that it never sang in a cage.

The man was furious and threatened that if the nightingale did not sing then he would kill it. "Oh, please don't kill me," the nightingale pleaded. "Set me free and I shall tell you three very valuable things which will prove more useful than me." The man opened the cage and the nightingale flew off to the branch of a tree. Then it said, "Never believe a captive's promise for he will deceive you. Second, learn to keep what you have and finally, don't cry over what is gone." Saying this, it flew away.

# 15 How the Rabbit Lost Its Tail

In olden times, rabbits had a long tail and short, straight legs.

One day in a forest, a rabbit found a man weeping. When the rabbit asked him why he was so sad, the man answered, "I have to reach the village across the forest as I am getting married this evening. But I have lost my way and don't know what to do." The kind-hearted rabbit said, "Follow me, I will show you the way." The man was very grateful and started following the rabbit, but on the way, he fell into a pit.

The rabbit put his long tail in the pit and asked the man to hold it. But as the rabbit tried to pull the man out, his tail broke. Then the rabbit lowered his hind legs into the pit. He told the man to hold his legs tight and said he would pull him out. This time the rabbit managed to pull the man out but his paws had become long. From that day on, rabbits have a small tail and hop on their long hind legs.

# 16 The Birds and the Hemp Seeds

A wise old swallow lived on a peepal tree along with many other young birds. One beautiful summer morning, they were all flying in the sky. Way down below, they saw a farmer planting hemp seeds on his farm. Now, this farmer used to make huge nets out of hemp creepers and used them to trap birds. The old swallow knew this and warned the other birds. The wise swallow told them to collect every seed that the farmer had sown otherwise they would be in deep trouble later. But the other birds were lazy. They did not heed his advice and continued to play all day. They did not pick up the hemp seeds.

After some months, the farmer made a net out of the hemp that had now grown into big plants. He cast the net in the jungle and all the birds except for the wise swallow were caught in it. They struggled to free themselves but the net was strong and they couldn't escape.

The wise swallow then said to them, "The net is made of the same hemp seeds I had asked you to pick when the farmer was sowing them. These have now grown and the farmer has made a net from its creepers to catch you. But you did not listen to me then."

The other birds realised what a big mistake they had made by not obeying the wise swallow.

# 17 The Brave Tailor

Once there lived a tailor. One day, he was sewing some new clothes when a bunch of flies started troubling him. He shooed them away, but they still continued to trouble him. The tailor then took a fly swatter and killed seven flies with one swat. "I have killed seven in a single blow!" shouted the tailor.

At this very moment, two ladies were standing outside his shop and talking about a fearsome giant. This giant was killing the people of the kingdom and eating them up. When they heard what the tailor said, the ladies thought that he was very brave and that he had killed seven giants in one blow! They ran to the king and told him about the brave tailor. "Bring him to me!" ordered the king. The tailor tried to explain that he had only killed seven flies but in vain. "Go, kill the giant!" the king ordered the tailor. The poor man had no choice but obey.

The tailor reached the giant's house. "What a mighty man! I can't kill him," he thought. Then the clever tailor had an idea. At night, while the giant was sleeping, he sewed the giant's mouth together! Now the giant could not eat anything. When he woke up, he begged the tailor to undo the stitches on his mouth. The tailor agreed to do so on one condition and said, "I will reopen your mouth only if you promise not to eat any more men from our kingdom!"

The giant agreed and the tailor undid the stitches. The giant left the kingdom and the tailor got a handsome reward from the king. Everyone lived happily ever after.

# 18 Thirteenth

Thirteenth was the youngest of thirteen brothers. There lived a monster in the forest nearby. One day, the king announced that whoever would bring the monster's blanket would be rewarded. Thirteenth went to the monster's house and found him sleeping. He pulled the blanket and ran back. He gave the quilt to the king and was well rewarded.

The king then announced that whoever brought the monster would marry the princess. Thirteenth disguised himself as a monk and went to the monster with a cage. He said, "I want to catch that boy Thirteenth in this cage." The monster said, "I will help you because he stole my blanket." The monk said, "I don't know if Thirteenth will fit in this cage. Let us see if you fit in the cage because if you can, so can Thirteenth." The monster agreed and entered the cage. Thirteenth locked the cage and took him to the king. The king was very pleased and married him to the princess.

# 19 The Salt Merchant

Once a peddler was going home with his ass after buying salt. His home was across the stream. When they reached the stream, the ass accidentally fell into the water. When he got up, his load had been reduced since the salt had dissolved in the water. This delighted the ass. Next time the peddler again loaded him with salt and this time the ass fell down on purpose. He got up again feeling his load lightened and brayed in triumph.

The peddler understood the ass's trick and decided to teach him a lesson. This time he loaded the ass with sponges instead of salt. So when the ass purposely fell down into the stream, he felt that his load had doubled as the sponges had become laden with water. Thus the ass's trick backfired on him.

# 20 The Old Witch

A poor girl was looking for work. She came across a cottage with a huge oven kept outside. To her surprise the oven said, "Please take the bread out, it is baked." The girl took the bread out and put it on the ground.

She saw that she had reached a witch's house. The witch kept her as a servant and made her work all day and all night. The witch warned her never to look up the chimney in the house. One day the girl was overcome by curiosity. "Why has the witch has forbidden me? Let me look." She found a bag of gold! She took it out and was about to run home with it when the witch returned. The oven said, "Quick! Hide behind me." Soon the witch came to the oven and asked, "Have you seen the girl pass by?" The oven said, "Look inside me."

As the witch bent to look inside the oven, she fell into it. She howled in pain and was burnt to death. The girl took the gold home and lived happily ever after.

## 21 The Queen of Hearts

Alice was wandering in Wonderland when she saw a white rose tree. Three gardeners, who were actually a pack of cards, were painting the roses red. "How strange. Everyone I meet here acts in a funny way. I wonder why?" Alice thought to herself. She asked politely, "Why you are painting the roses?" The gardeners bowed low to her and said, "You see, we planted a white rose tree by mistake. The queen will have our heads cut off if she finds out." Just then the Queen of Hearts came by in a grand procession. She looked at the rose tree and after checking it, shrieked, "Off with their heads!" Alice hid the frightened gardeners in a flowerpot and saved their lives. She left the gardeners and continued her journey through lands where she had many more adventures.

## 22 The Strange Old Man

One day, a kind boy called Dummling went to the forest to collect wood. There, he met a strange man who begged him for food. Dummling shared his food with the old man. Then the man asked him to help him cut a tree. Dummling obediently cut the tree and to his surprise found a magical golden goose inside it. The man gave him the goose as a repayment for his help. Dummling returned home happily.

On his way, he met a beautiful princess and fell in love with her. "If you drink all the wine in my cellar, you may marry her," said the king. Dummling went to the strange man in the forest for help. That night, the man went to the cellar and secretly drank all the wine. Then the king said, "I want you to find a ship that can sail both on land and water." Once again the man helped Dummling build such a ship. At last the king had to agree to marry the princess and Dummling.

## 23 Snow White Fire Red

"When our first child is born I will build two fountains, one of oil and one of wine," declared the king. Soon, the queen gave birth to a son and true to his word, the king kept his promise. After seven years, the fountains began to dry up. A witch had been collecting oil from the fountains, drop by drop.

One day, the prince was playing with his friends. He threw a ball and broke the pitcher of oil. The furious witch cursed the prince saying, "You will never marry anyone!" The king begged the witch to take back her curse and at last she said, "You will marry only Snow White Fire Red."

When the prince was eighteen, he set out looking for Snow White Fire Red. One day, he found a witch standing below the balcony of a big castle. "Snow White Fire Red, lower your hair," she said. A beautiful girl lowered her long hair and the witch climbed up. When the witch left the next day, the prince stood below the balcony and said, "Snow White Fire Red, lower your hair." He then climbed up to the balcony. "Who are you?" asked the prince. "I am a princess of the neighbouring state. The wicked witch is keeping me a captive," said the girl. "Quick! Let's leave before the witch comes back," said the prince. He helped the princess climb down. They sat on the waiting horse and galloped away as fast as they could.

His father and mother were very happy to see them. They invited the neighbouring king and queen. The prince and Snow White Fire Red were married in great splendour.

## 24 The Duck with Red Feet

Once there lived a hunter. He had a brother who was red-complexioned and was so small that he lived in a small box.

One day, the hunter married. But he did not tell his wife about his little brother. Every night he would keep aside half the food and give it to his little brother when his wife was asleep. His wife became curious and wondered what he did with the food. One night, she pretended to sleep and saw her husband giving the food to the little red man. Next morning when her husband went hunting, she opened the box and brought the little brother out. But he was so frightened that he slipped out of her hands and ran out of the door.

When the hunter returned, he saw his wife's red hands and found his brother missing. He was very angry and ran after her with a stick. She jumped into a river and became a Sheldrake duck. That is why till today, the Sheldrake ducks have red feet.

# 25 The Horned Witches

One day, while a woman was spinning yarn in her house, there was a knock at the door. When she opened the door, twelve witches entered the house.

The first witch had one horn on her head, the second witch had two horns and so on. They were very ugly. The witches sat down and started spinning. They gave the frightened woman a sieve and ordered her to bring water from the well nearby. The woman went to the well and tried to fill the sieve but the water wouldn't stay in it. The poor woman was even more scared of what the witches might do to her.

Then the well spoke, "Plaster the sieve with clay. Take it to the house and shout that there is a fire in Slievenamon. Slievenamon is the place where the witches live."

The woman did as she was told. When the witches heard her, they were terrified and ran away, never to be seen again.

# 26 The Thieves and the Cock

One night, some thieves entered a house. But they couldn't find anything worth stealing except an old cock. They took it away with them. "Let us kill the cock so that we can at least have a good meal," said one thief.

As they were about to cut his head, the cock pleaded, "Please don't kill me! I am very useful to man. Every morning I crow and wake people up. Please have mercy." The thieves were taken aback to hear the cock speak. Then another thief said, "By waking people up early, you make stealing difficult for us. It is because of you that our livelihood is spoilt. We have all the more reason to kill you." Saying this, the thieves cut off the head of the cock and put him in a pot over the fire.

The poor cock was foolish enough to get killed by his own argument.

## 27 Dick Whittington and His Cat

Dick Whittington was a poor scullery boy in Mr. Fitz Warren's huge mansion.

He stayed in a little room, which was filled with rats. They ate his food and chewed his clothes. "I must buy a cat who will kill all the rats," he thought. In a few days the cat killed the rats. Dick and the cat became good friends.

Mr. Warren was a rich trader. One of his ships was leaving London with goods to trade. He said to Dick, "You must give something you have which can be traded for money or gold." Poor Dick only had his cat but gave him away to his master with a heavy heart.

A few days later Mr. Warren received a letter from the King of Barbary. But lo! It was addressed to Dick. "The king will gift Dick a bag full of diamonds for sending his cat to get rid of the rats in the king's palace," read Mr Warren. So Dick Whittington became a rich man and he also got back his cat!

## 28 Ali and the Sultan

Once there was a man named Ali. He was very funny and was always making fun of the sultan. Everybody knew about Ali's jokes and the sultan himself, came to know about them. The sultan was very angry and called Ali to the palace. Clever Ali, on reaching the palace, began to sing the sultan's praises. He loudly praised the sultan's looks, wealth, and power. The pleased ruler then said to Ali, "Wonderful! You have made me very happy! As a reward you can choose one of these beautiful saddles!" When Ali returned with a donkey's saddle on his back, everybody asked him what the sultan had said. Ali winked and replied, "The sultan was so pleased that he gave me one of his own robes to wear!" Everyone burst out laughing.

## 29 The Corn Plants

Once upon a time there was a tribe on an island. A warrior of the tribe lived by the seashore. His job was to inform his people whenever enemies came to the island. Though the warrior caught fish he never had enough to eat.

One day, he came to a land that was red in colour. There he saw a little man who said, "I challenge you to wrestle with me. If you are able to throw me on the ground, you will never have any shortage of food."

The warrior agreed and threw him on the ground. As soon as the little man fell, he disappeared and a strange fruit appeared in his place. A voice came from inside the fruit, "Open my cover, scatter the seeds on the plains and come back in summer." The warrior did as he was told.

When the warrior came back in summer, he found many corn plants growing in the same place. He plucked the corn, ground the seeds, and made bread. Now he had enough food.

## 30 The Australian Grasshopper

Once a scientist went to Australia for the first time. There, he was amazed to see a kangaroo because he had never seen one before. He threw a stone at it and the kangaroo jumped away.

The scientist wanted to ask the guide about the animal but didn't want to sound foolish and ignorant. So he thought for a while and then asked, "Are the grasslands in Australia very big?" The guide answered, "No, they are as big as they are in England and America."

Then the scientist said, " I think the grass that you purchase for your horses must be fifty feet tall." The guide replied in surprise, "Not at all, it is only a few inches long."

Then the scientist pointed towards the kangaroo and asked, "I was wondering about the unusual size of that grasshopper." The guide had a good laugh.

# 31 The Little Pine Tree

In a forest grew a little pine tree. It felt quite lonely, as there were no other pine trees around and it had no friends. It also felt sad because it had long needles instead of leaves.

One night, it wished that it had leaves of gold. When it woke up in the morning, it found that the wish had come true and it had golden leaves now. The pine tree was very happy to see its gold leaves sparkling in the sunlight. Soon a woodcutter came to the forest. He plucked all the gold leaves and took them away. The pine tree was sad and wished it had leaves of glass so that no one would take them.

Next morning, its wish had been fulfilled and it had leaves of glass. The pine tree was happy again and was delighted to hear its glass leaves tinkling when the wind blew. But, there was a big storm in the afternoon and all the glass leaves shattered and fell on the ground.

The pine tree was sad again and wished it had big green leaves. The pine tree was very happy the next morning, as its wish had come true for the third time. But soon a goat came and ate each one of the leaves.

The pine tree now wished he could get his long needles back. And was very happy the next morning when it got its needles back. He thought to himself, "Gold leaves, glass leaves, and green leaves are all fine but only long needles are good for a little pine tree like me."

# Contents

*The Story of the Month:  Beauty and the Beast*

The Story of the Month

# Beauty and the Beast

## Beauty and the Beast

Once upon a time there lived a wealthy merchant and his three daughters.

One day, the father was to go to a far-off place and he asked his daughters what they wanted on his return. The first and the second daughter asked for lovely dresses. But the third daughter, whose name was Beauty, said, "Father, I only need a rose plucked by your hand." The merchant, on his way back, had to cross through the deep forest. It was dark and the merchant tried to find a place to sleep. He suddenly found a huge castle and went inside to find no-body. There was a huge

table with delicious food and he ate it all. Then the merchant went into the bedroom and slept on a soft and fluffy bed. The next day, too, the merchant did not find anyone in the castle. He saw a beautiful rose bush growing in the lawn and remembered Beauty's gift. He plucked a red rose from the bush.

Suddenly, a ferocious looking beast sprang out of the bush. He was wearing fine silk clothes and roared, "I gave you food and a bed to sleep in! And now, you are stealing my roses!" The merchant was frightened and told the Beast about Beauty's gift. The Beast decided to let him go only if he

promised to send Beauty to this castle. The merchant agreed and ran back home. He cried and told his daughters about the Beast. But Beauty loved her father a lot and agreed to go stay with the Beast.

The Beast treated Beauty with a lot of kindness. He was never rude to her. He let her stay in the biggest room and let her roam in the beautiful garden. Beauty would sit near the fireplace and sew while the Beast kept her company. At first, Beauty was afraid of the Beast but slowly, she began to like him.

One day, the Beast asked Beauty to marry him, but she refused. She was still afraid of his fearful-looking face. The Beast still treated her kindly and with a lot of love. Beauty missed her father a lot. The Beast gave her a magic mirror and said, "Look at the mirror and you can see your family. Now you won't feel lonely anymore."

One day, Beauty looked in the mirror and saw that father was very ill and dying. She went to the Beast and pleaded and cried, "Please let me go home! I only want to see my father be- fore he dies!" But the Beast roared, "No! You promised you would never leave this castle!" Saying this, he stormed out of the room. But after some time, he came to Beauty and said, "You may go to stay with your father for seven days. But you must promise to return after that." Beauty was very happy and agreed. Then she left and went to stay with her father. Her father, on seeing Beauty, felt very happy and soon recov- ered. Beauty stayed with her family for seven days and more. She forgot the Beast and his castle. But one night, she had a terrible nightmare in which she saw the Beast was very ill and about to die. He was crying, "Beauty, please come back!"

Beauty woke up and went back to the castle because she did not mean to hurt the Beast. She cried and said, "Please don't die, Beast! I will live with you forever!" The Beast mirac- ulously changed into a hand- some prince. He said, "I was under a curse all these years and could only be relieved when someone fell in love with me. I am now cured of the curse because you truly love me." And then, Beauty and the Beast were married and together they lived happily ever after.

# 1 Fearless John

Fearless John was a young man who feared nothing.

One day, the king announced that he would marry his daughter, the beautiful Princess Lily of the Valley to anyone who dared to spend the night in the haunted woods.

Fearless John decided to try his luck in marrying the princess. He went to the woods, where he saw a castle, deep inside the jungle. This castle was actually haunted and was called the Castle of Terror.

That night, just as he was about to sleep he heard a big commotion. He saw many ghosts approaching him. But Fearless John was not worried. He picked up a club and chased them all away.

The next night, Fearless John saw an enormous bear in the castle. But John was not worried. He tied the beast up. On the third night, Fearless John came face-to-face with a fire-breathing dragon in the Castle of Terror. But John was still not worried. He made the monster run up and down, in and out. The dragon ran round and round until he was dizzy and collapsed and fell to the floor. John dragged the dragon into a well.

On the fourth day, Fearless John returned home. When the king heard about Fearless John's adventures and how he had stayed in the Castle of Terror, he was impressed.

The king announced the marriage of Fearless John and his daughter, Princess Lily of the Valley. News of John's bravery spread far and wide and all the people rejoiced with the royal family.

# 2 The Wooden Calf

Once a man made a calf out of wood. The wooden calf could move its tail and head and almost looked like a real calf. The man was silly enough to think that the calf would become big one day. He told a shepherd to take it to graze.

He asked the shepherd to carry the calf to the meadow as it was too small to walk on its own. The shepherd was also foolish. He put the calf with the other cows out on the grass.

In the evening, when the calf was nowhere to be seen, the shepherd thought that it must have walked back on its own and came back empty-handed. The owner was very angry and blamed the shepherd for losing his calf.

The matter was taken to the judge and the judge gave his decision in favour of the owner. The shepherd was asked to give him a cow as compensation for losing the wooden calf. That's how a wooden calf became a real cow.

## 3 The Bags Full of Faults

There is a Greek legend that says that when man was created, the father of the gods, Zeus, decided to give him two bags.

One bag contained the man's own negative qualities while the other contained everybody else's faults. Zeus hung these bags on a long pole. But he made a mistake because of which man is today what he is today. And do you want to know what that mistake was?

Zeus hung the bag that had other people's faults on the front end of the pole while the bag that contained man's own faults was hung further behind. So man was able to see other's defects before he could see his own.

This is the reason why we tend to see the faults of others while we are hardly able to see our own.

## 4 The Fighting Cocks

On a cold, rainy day, a farmer found two chicks near his door. The chicks were miserable and shivering. The farmer took them inside. He decided to keep them and made a wooden coop for them to live in. Soon, the chicks grew up and became cocks. They were very lazy and kept fighting with each other.

One day, they had a big fight about who was the ruler of the coop. One of the cocks ran out of the coop and hid in the farmer's house. The other cock was very proud that he had the coop to himself. He climbed on top of it and crowed loudly to show his leadership.

Suddenly, the neighbouring cat pounced on him and ate him up. The cat had been watching and knew that the other cock was inside the house. He hid near the door.

After a while, when the cock came out of the house to go back to the coop, the cat jumped and killed it too. Both the cocks died because of their own folly.

## 5 The Moon and Mother Fairy

One night Little Moon said to her mother, "Mother, please make me a beautiful gown like the one you are wearing." Mother Fairy replied, "My child, there are no gowns which will fit you." Little Moon was upset. She wanted to look as beautiful as her mother. "But, Mother, you are a fairy and you can create anything," implored Little Moon. "Can't you make me a gown?"

"Sure I could," said Mother Fairy, "but what do I do with a child who is at one time a New Moon, at another a Full Moon and at other times not there at all!" Little Moon started crying, so Mother Fairy explained to her, "Oh, but you are the prettiest thing in the sky and a gown will only hide your beauty." Little Moon beamed happily.

## 6 Straw, Coal and the Bean

Once an old woman had gathered beans to make food for herself. She lit a fire and put some straw in it. She was about to put the beans in the pan, when one bean jumped out and sat beside a piece of straw, which was left outside. A burning piece of coal also leapt out from the fire and joined them.

They considered themselves lucky to have escaped death and decided to go to a foreign country where they could live safely. They left the house. Soon, they reached a little brook and didn't know how to cross it. So the straw laid itself across the banks and told the others to use it as a bridge.

No sooner did the coal start crossing, the straw was unable to bear the load and fell into the river along with the coal. But the bean was safe. It had such a hearty laugh that it split into two.

A tailor who was passing by saw the bean and sewed it together with a black thread. That is why beans have a black seam.

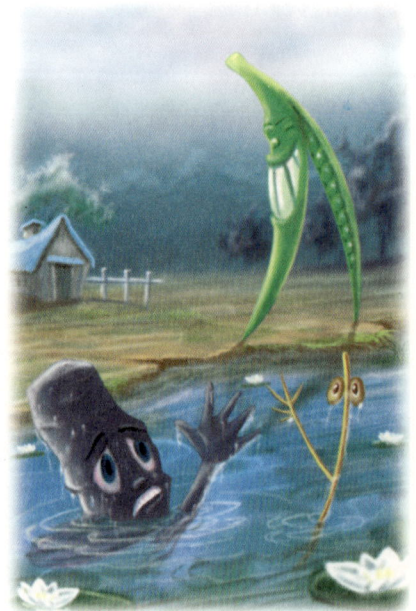

## 7 The Six Swans

There lived a king who once lost his way while hunting in the forest. He met an old woman who said, " I will show you the way out on the condition that you marry my daughter." The king agreed.

The king had six sons and one daughter. He was worried that his new queen would not treat his children well. "I will not tell her about the children. I will hide them in the castle."

Meanwhile, the suspicious queen who was actually a witch, bribed the servants and found out the secret way to the castle. She reached the castle and with her magical powers, turned the six boys into swans.

The little sister was left to wander alone in the forest. One day, she saw the swans and recognised her brothers. "If you sew six shirts of starflowers for us within six years we will be free. But you cannot utter a word or laugh even during this time," they said.

Years passed by. Meanwhile, the king of the neighbouring country came hunting to the forest. He was captivated by her beauty and married her. The king had a wicked mother who was not happy with this marriage. She convinced the king that the new queen tried to kill her own children. She forced him to sentence the queen to death by the fire. The queen was unable to speak in her defense. Just when the fire was about to be lit, six swans came flying towards her, touched the shirts and became free from enchantment. They regained their human forms and told the entire story to the king. The king punished the wicked mother for her treachery. The brothers and sister were overjoyed to be united.

## 8 Clever Grethel

Once there was a cook called Grethel. "I have a new guest coming to dinner tonight. I want you to prepare two chickens in his honour," said her master. The tempting aroma of cooking made Grethel's mouth water. When the guest was late in coming, the master went out to look for him. Unable to control her greed, Grethel ate up the chickens. She was just wiping her lips when the master arrived "My guest is coming in a while," he announced.

Now Grethel was worried and wondered how to save herself. She waited for the guest at the door. When he came, she whispered in his ears, "Oh, sir! My master is very angry. He is going to cut off both your ears to punish you for arriving late." On hearing this, the guest ran away in fear, never to be seen again. Grethel told her master that his guest had run away with both the chickens. The angry master cursed the guest. Clever Grethel peacefully went to sleep.

## 9 The Herdsman and the Lost Bull

Once a herdsman was tending to his flock in the forest when he realised that he had lost a bull calf. He searched long and hard for it everywhere but could not find it. Finally, he vowed that if he could find the thief who had stolen his calf he would be very grateful and would sacrifice a lamb to the guardian deities of the forest—Hermes and Pan.

Some time later, while climbing up a small hillock, he saw a lion eating his lost calf. He was terrified that the lion would kill him too and raising his hands in despair, he declared, "Athough I vowed just now that I would offer a sacrifice to the gods of the forest if I found the robber of my bull calf, but now I promise that I will add a fat bull in addition to my calf to please the guardian deities if I can safely get away from here."

## 10 The Hare's Friends

A hare had many friends. One day, she heard some hounds approaching, but she thought her friends would definitely save her. She first went to the horse for help but he declined to carry the hare on his back saying that he had important work to do for his master.

The hare was sure that his other friends would help him. The bull said, "I'm sorry. I have an appointment with a lady but am sure the goat will help you." But the goat feared that her back might hurt. And the ram was scared that the hounds would eat him up.

Finally, the hare requested the calf to rescue him, but the calf did not want to do something which the elders had declined to do. By then the hounds were very near. The hare took to her heels and fled.

The hare had learnt her lesson. One good friend is worth many false friends.

## 11 The Wooden God

Once upon a time there lived a priest called Andre. He was a great believer in God. He used to worship a wooden idol every day and also burn incense for him.

But he remained very poor. Good fortune had never knocked on his door. Then one day, angry and dejected, he smashed the wooden god. Lo and behold! A vast number of coins fell out from the statue.

## 12 The Mouse, the Bird and the Sausage

A bird, a mouse and a sausage lived together. The bird was in charge of getting wood from the forest every day, the mouse had to get water and make the fire and the sausage was in charge of cooking.

They lived happily until one day the bird met another bird who told him that his work was the most difficult while his other friends had easy jobs. Now the bird refused to go to the forest the next day and demanded that they should exchange their work. The mouse and the sausage were against this proposal but they were forced to agree to the bird's wish.

Alas! Everything went wrong. When the sausage went to cut wood, it slipped down from the tree and was eaten up by a dog, the mouse burned itself and perished while cooking and the bird fell into the well and drowned.

## 13 Catherine and the Golden Coins

Catherine was a dull and stupid woman. Her husband tried hard to make her clever but failed. One day, he had to go away for a few days.

Before leaving, he put some gold coins in a box and buried it in the garden. He told Catherine that he was burying a box of sunflower seeds.

After a few days, some pot sellers came to the village. They showed the pots to Catherine. She liked them but had no money to buy them.

Suddenly, Catherine had an idea. She remembered the sunflower seeds and asked the pot sellers if they would exchange their pots for her sunflower seeds. They were curious to see the seeds, so she told them to dig out the box that her husband had buried.

The pot sellers were happy to walk away with the gold coins!

# 14 The Brave Cub

Once upon a time a lion was walking through the woods with his lioness and their two cubs. All of a sudden, the cubs fell into a trap laid by the hunters. The parents desperately tried to free them. They peered into the trap. It was very dark and deep. They thought that the cubs would never be able to get out of it so they sat outside and consoled the cubs.

But the cubs kept on trying to jump out of the ditch. After some time, one of them got tired and gave up after he heard his mother say how deep the trap was.

Meanwhile, the other cub kept trying hard and finally was able to leap out of the trap and save himself. This little cub was deaf and could not hear his parents' words of consolation. Instead, all the while he thought that his parents had been encouraging him to jump out and that had spurred him to keep trying hard and finally make his way out of the trap.

# 15 The Jay and the Peacocks

One day, a jay entered a yard where peacocks roamed.

There he found lovely peacock feathers on the ground. The jay thought that he would look very pretty if he tied the feathers to his body. So he tied all the feathers to his tail and flew towards the peacocks who were dancing in merriment. They were angry at what the jay had done and called him a cheat.

They decided to teach him a lesson. They pecked him and plucked away his plumes. The jay felt embarrassed at what he had done. The other birds were also looking at him and laughing.

He went back to the other jays who were very annoyed with him for his silly behaviour. They said that he had brought disgrace to all other the jays and advised him, "Only by having pretty feathers you can't be a fine bird."

# 16 Pinocchio's Last Adventure

"Let's go to Toyland. No one has to study there and we can play all day!" said Carlo, a boy in Pinocchio's class. Forgetting his promises to his father, Gepetto, Pinocchio went with him. When they reached Toyland, they turned into donkeys! That's what happened to boys in Toyland. But Pinocchio was too excited to mind.

Then alas! The Toyland wagon driver wanted Pinocchio the donkey's skin. He threw Pinocchio in the sea waiting for him to die. "Help," shouted poor Pinocchio. Before he knew it a shark had swallowed him. Frightened, he crawled inside the huge stomach of the shark. Suddenly, he spied a light ahead. To his joy he saw it was Gepetto. Gepetto had been looking for Pinocchio at sea when the shark swallowed his boat. Father and son hugged joyfully. When the shark was asleep they crept out through its open mouth. From that day on Pinocchio worked hard helping his father, and the Turquoise Fairy turned him into a real boy!

# 17 The Wolf and the Seven Kids

Once there lived a goat with her seven kids. A big bad wolf lived near their house and always tried to catch the little kids. One day, the goat had to go out. She said to the kids, "Do not let anyone in, especially the wolf."

After she left, the wolf came and knocked on the door and said, "Let me in!" But the kids recognised his rough voice and refused to open the door. After a while, the wolf came again and knocked on the door. This time he spoke softly but the kids asked him to show his paws. When they saw his black paws on the windowsill they knew it was the wolf and did not let him in.

So, the wolf went to the baker and put some white flour on his paws. When he knocked on the door the third time, the kids saw the white paws and thought it was their mother.

As soon as they opened the door, the wolf gobbled up all the kids except for the youngest kid. "Momma, the wicked wolf has gobbled all my brothers!" sobbed the youngest kid when the goat came home. "I will teach that wolf a lesson," said the angry goat. She went to the sleeping wolf and cut his stomach. Out sprang all the six kids. They filled the wolf's stomach with stones and sewed him up.

When the wolf woke up and went to the well to drink water, the weight of the stones pulled him into the well and he was drowned.

## 18 The Travelling Companion

Once there lived a boy called John. One night while John was sleeping, his dead father appeared in his dreams and told him that he would win the loveliest bride in the world.

John left home to see the world. In a church, he saw two men trying to take a dead man out of a coffin because he had died without paying the money he owed to them. John paid the fifty dollars the man had borrowed and asked them to let the man rest in peace.

A little later, along the way, John met a man who became his travelling companion.

After a few days, they reached a town where they heard about the king's beautiful daughter who used to behead any suitor who failed to answer her three questions correctly. John recognized her as the woman he had seen in his dreams and decided to be her suitor.

Meanwhile, his companion came to know that the princess was under the spell of a wicked sorcerer. With the help of a swan's wings, the companion made himself invisible and went to the princess. He overheard the questions and answers that the sorcerer told the princess to ask. Then he beat up the sorcerer and beheaded him with his sword. He went to John and told him all the correct answers.

The next day, John gave the correct replies to the princess's questions and freed her from the sorcerer's spell. They were married and lived happily ever after. In the meantime, the travelling companion revealed himself as the dead man in the coffin. That was how he showed his gratitude to John.

## 19 The Tiger and the Woodpecker

Onc day a bone got stuck in a tiger's teeth while he was eating some flesh. He tried hard to remove it but could not. Helpless, he started roaring in pain.

A woodpecker sitting nearby saw the tiger's discomfort and asked what the matter was. The tiger pointed to the bone stuck in his teeth. The woodpecker promised to remove the bone from his teeth on the condition that the tiger would always give him a portion of his food. The tiger agreed and the woodpecker took out the bone with its sharp beak.

One day, the tiger had caught a fat prey and the woodpecker asked for his share. The tiger refused and said, "You should be thankful that I did not kill you when you entered my mouth." The woodpecker was enraged at the ungrateful tiger. He struck the tiger in one eye with his beak. The tiger roared with pain and the woodpecker said, "You should be thankful that I didn't blind both your eyes."

## 20 The Gardener and the Good King

There was a gardener who tended his garden passionately. He loved all his vegetables and flowers. His vegetables were very tasty and famous throughout the kingdom. His garden was a delight for onlookers. One day, a hare broke into his garden and damaged the plants and the vegetables. The gardener tried to chase it away but every day the hare would plunder his garden. At last, the gardener went to the king for help. The king sent his army to the garden. There was a feast before the search for the hare began. The hare was found at last but the king's hunters had done more damage to the garden than a hundred hares could have done. And the poor gardener wept and wondered, "Ah! Will my garden ever be the same again?"

## 21 The Pen and the Inkstand

A famous poet had a pen and an inkstand. The pen and the inkstand used to continuously fight as to who was the greatest of the two.

The inkstand thought that if it was not for him, men would never have produced such great verses and become famous. The pen argued that the inkstand was only the raw material. "The real work is done by me, for only when I write do beautiful lines fill up a page," insisted the pen. The two argued all the time.

One day, the poet came and wrote some lines on a paper, "How stupid is a violin and a bow for both claim that they made the music, when actually someone else composed it! How often do men boast of taking credit for their creations, forgetting that they are all actually instruments in the hands of the biggest creator—God!"

However the pen and the inkstand were very foolish and did not understand the true meaning of the lines and continued to fight forever.

## 22 Christmas

"Christmas is approaching. You must clean the house well," said Jack to his wife. The silly wife thought that Christmas must be a man. "Are you Christmas?" she asked all the people passing by. One wily person, who was going down the street, said that his name was Christmas. The silly wife gave him everything inside the house. When her husband came to know of this, he was very angry.

"Be careful this time. Keep the pig for Christmas," warned Jack. The stupid woman called the man who called himself Christmas and gave him the pig. When her husband came home and asked her about the pig, she said, "But you told me to give it to Christmas!" He held his head in despair and vowed never to say anything to her.

## 23 King Thrushbeard

A king had a very beautiful daughter who was very arrogant. She thought that no man was good enough for her.

Once she ridiculed one of her suitors saying, "His chin is like a thrush's beak." From that day the poor suitor was called Thrushbeard.

The king was very angry with his daughter. "You are not fit be a princess. As a punishment you will marry a beggar." The beggar sent her to work as a maid in the king's kitchen. At the ceremony of the prince's wedding, she stood watching all the people gaily dancing. The princess felt sad alone.

Suddenly, the prince asked her to dance with him. He told her that he was Thrushbeard, the same suitor whom she had ridiculed in the past. He also told her that he had disguised himself as the beggar to teach her a lesson. "Please forgive me. Now I know I was wrong," begged the princess. Thrushbeard was kind. He forgave her and they lived happily ever after.

## 24 The Twelve Dancing Princesses

Once upon a time there was a king who had twelve beautiful daughters. The strange thing about them was that every morning their shoes were found to be worn off as if they had been dancing all night.

The king was puzzled and announced that whoever would find out where the princesses went every night could marry anyone of them. Many kings came to try their luck but they all failed to find the secret. An old soldier heard about this and decided to try his luck. He went to a sorceress, who gave him a cloak that would make him invisible. She also warned him not to drink the wine, which one of the princesses would bring for him.

Then the soldier went to the king. The king received him with full honour. At night, a feast was organised where the princesses served wine to him. He secretly threw away the wine and pretended to be asleep. The princesses, thinking that the soldier was asleep, went underground through a trap door. The soldier put on the cloak that would make him invisible and followed the princesses. He saw the princesses entering a beautiful garden.

Then, twelve princes came in twelve boats and took the princesses to a castle across the lake where they all danced the whole night till their shoes were worn. The soldier saw the same happenings three nights in a row.

On the fourth day, he told the king about the place where the princesses went every night. As proof, he showed one of the golden cups from which they drank wine. As his reward, he chose to marry the eldest princess.

## 25 Old Sultan

A farmer had a faithful dog called Sultan. But when Sultan grew old, the ungrateful farmer decided to shoot it.

Sultan overheard this and went to the wolf for help. They made a plan. One day, the wolf pretended to carry away the farmer's child but Sultan rescued the child as had been planned. The farmer was grateful and didn't kill Sultan. In return, the wolf asked Sultan to pretend to close his eyes when he would come to steal his master's sheep. But Sultan remained loyal to his master and refused. The wolf challenged him to a fight. The wild boar was called to be the witness.

This time clever Sultan went with a cat, which had only three legs. When the wolf and the boar saw the cat walking on three legs, they were scared of the strange creature and climbed up a tree to hide. But a little later they realised their folly. The wolf was ashamed for showing such fear and made peace with Sultan.

## 26 The Wolf and the Man

Once a fox was telling a wolf how strong man was and how difficult it was for an animal to overcome him. But the wolf boasted that if he could see a man, he would attack him at once and kill him.

The next day, the fox showed the wolf a hunter who was carrying a gun and a sword. The wolf attacked the hunter, but the hunter took his gun and fired back at him. The boastful wolf faced him bravely. Then the hunter fired another shot at the wolf. Though in pain, the wolf continued to fight with the hunter. This time the hunter used his sword and gave the wolf a few blows. Bleeding and howling, the wolf ran back to the fox and told him what had happened.

The fox gently told the wolf that he was boastful and that was why he was suffering now. The wolf had learnt his lesson.

## 27 The Basket of Mangoes

Judith was a very untidy girl. "Judith, you must keep your room tidy," her mother was tired of telling her.

One day, her friend brought a basket of mangoes for her as Judith loved mangoes. Since her room was in a mess as usual, Judith kept the mangoes on a chair.

She returned tired to her room after her evening play. Not finding any empty place to sit, she sat down on the nearest chair. "Squash! Squelch!" She jumped up and gave a cry of shock. She realised that she had sat on the mangoes! Her mother came running to her room on hearing her shout.

To her dismay, she saw that all the mangoes were crushed. "Oh, my favourite dress is spoilt! Mummy, what shall I do?" "That is why I always tell you to keep your room clean," said Mummy.

From that day, Judith learnt to keep her things in order.

## 28 The Cabbage

One day, two boys, Tom and Harry, were passing by a garden. They saw a big cabbage and Tom boasted, "I once saw a cabbage bigger than this." Harry promptly replied, "That must have been huge. Once I made a pot bigger than the church." Tom was puzzled. "Why?" he asked. "To boil your cabbage," replied Harry. Tom was ashamed and realised that he must not tell lies.

## 29 The Arab and His Camel

It was a cold winter night. An Arab was resting in his tent when his camel peeped inside and asked, "Master, it's very cold outside. Please allow me to put my head inside your tent."

The kind master took pity on the poor animal and agreed to the camel's request. A little later, the camel asked, "Master, please let me put my neck inside your tent as well." Once again the master allowed him to do so.

Next, the camel asked if he could put his forelegs in and again the kind master agreed. Very soon, the camel was completely inside the tent. But the tent was too small for both the master and the camel.

Finally, the camel asked his master to leave the tent so that he could be more comfortable. By now the master was very angry and turned the camel out in the cold again.

## 30 The Death of the Little Hen

Once a little hen and a little cock were eating nuts. But a nut got stuck in the hen's throat.

The cock rushed to fetch water for her from a well nearby. But the well told him to bring him some red silk from a bride before he could take out any water. The cock went to the bride, who told him to bring her a wreath.

The cock finally brought water for the hen. But it was too late. The hen was already dead.

A carriage pulled by six mice was built to carry the hen to the grave. On the way, they had to cross a stream. When they reached the stream, a straw, a coal and a stone tried to help them to cross but they all slipped and drowned in the stream. The cock managed to reach the other side and buried the hen. But he was heartbroken without his friend and soon died.

# Contents

*The Story of the Month:   Little Mermaid*

The Story of the Month

# Little Mermaid

# Little Mermaid

Long long ago, in the Deep Sea kingdom, there lived the sea king with his five mermaid daughters. Sirenetta was the youngest and the loveliest among them. She had a beautiful voice and everybody from far and wide came to hear her sing and praised her voice and her beauty.

One day, while Sirenetta was swimming on the surface of the water and watching ships go by, she saw a young man falling off his ship. She swam swiftly to save him from drowning and dragged him to the shore. Soon, people found the man on the shore and Sirenetta swam

away. This man was actually the prince of a kingdom. When he became conscious, the prince looked around for the girl who had saved him but no one knew who she was.

Sirenetta often thought of the young man and fell in love with the prince, but she was sad because she could never be like all the other ladies he knew. They had two feet and she had a fish tail!

In the Deep Sea lived a witch with magical powers. One day, Sirenetta went to beg her for human legs. The witch said, "I need your beautiful voice! Only then I shall give you legs! But

you must remember, every time you set your feet on the ground, it will hurt very badly!" Sirenetta agreed. She did not mind the pain. All she wanted was to be with the prince. As soon as she got her two feet Sirenetta became dumb. When she was leaving, the witch said, "If your prince marries anybody else, you shall dissolve in the sea water. You can never become a mermaid again!"

With the witch's magic spell, Sirenetta found herself lying on the beach and the prince looking down at her. He asked, "Where are you

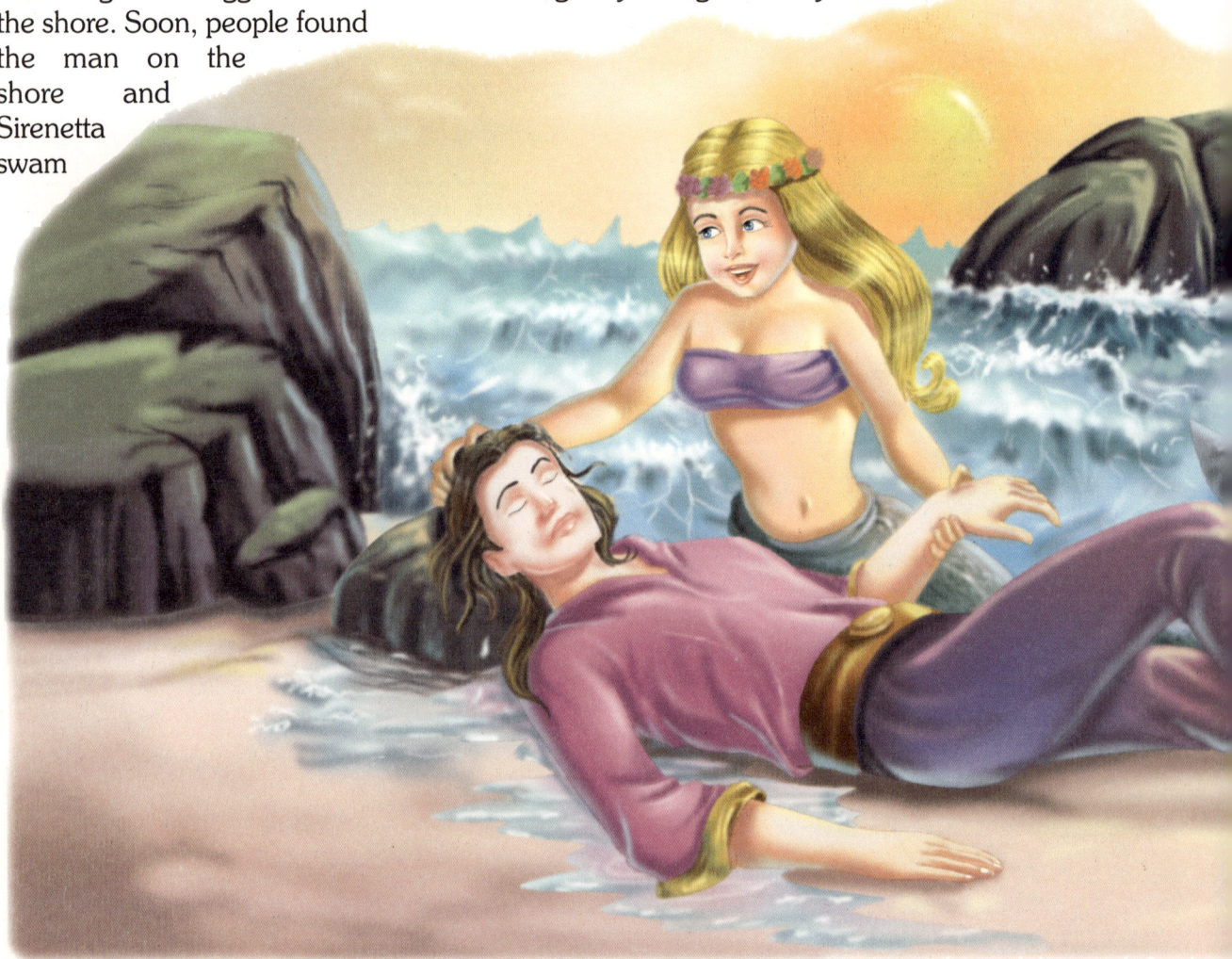

from?" But she could not reply. The prince took her to his palace and looked after her. They became good friends and had a wonderful time together. Every step Sirenetta took hurt, but she bore it all silently. She loved the prince but the prince was in love with the beautiful maiden who had saved him. The prince did not realise it had been Sirenetta and she couldn't tell him.

Obeying the wishes of his father, the prince went to meet the daughter of a neighbouring king. Enchanted by her beauty the prince was convinced this was the same maiden who rescued him. He

asked the princess to marry him. A grand wedding took place.

Sirenetta was heartbroken. That night, crying she ran to the seashore. There she saw four mermaids. Why, they were her sisters! One of them handed her a knife and said, "Here, Sirenetta! This is a magic knife! We gave our long hair locks to the witch of the Deep Sea and she gave this to us in return. Kill your prince and you shall turn into a mermaid again! Then you can come and live with us!"

Sirenetta took the magic knife and went to the prince's

room at night. But she loved him so much that she could not kill him. She knew that at dawn, she would vanish into the sea, just as the witch of the Deep Sea had told her earlier. She sat on the shore and wept silently.

Suddenly, from the sky came a pink cloud. It lifted her from the land into the sky. "Where am I?" asked Sirenetta, for now she could talk. The beautiful fairies replied, "We are the air fairies. You are now one of us because you did a good deed for the person you love. Come with us."

From then on, the little mermaid, Sirenetta, lived in the sky with the fairies.

# 1 The Cat and the Mouse

Once, a cat and a mouse were very good friends and happily lived together in the same house. As winter was approaching, they decided to stock some food items. So they went to the market and bought a big pot of cheese.

Fearing that other cats and mice might steal their cheese, they hid it behind the altar in the church.

The cat was very greedy. After a few days, he had a great yearning to taste the cheese. He went to the mouse and told him that he was invited to baptize his cousin's child in the church. The mouse believed him and the cat set out for his first steal.

He ate a large chunk of the cheese and returned home happily. When the mouse asked him what the child was named the cat replied, "Top-off." The mouse was surprised at the name.

After a few days the greedy cat wanted to have some cheese again and told the mouse that he had to baptize another child and rushed to the church. He finished half the cheese and told the mouse that this time the child was named "Half-gone."

After a few days, the cat made the same excuse and went again and finished the remaining cheese. This time he told the mouse that the child was named "All-gone." The mouse was puzzled by the cat's behaviour but did not say anything.

When winter came, the mouse went to the church to get the cheese but found that it had vanished. At last he understood the trick played by the greedy cat.

# 2 The White Snake

A man used to eat a strange dish after dinner every day. His servant noticed it and became curious. One day he peeped into the dish. To his astonishment, he found a white snake! He took a bite to taste it. Lo! He found that he could now understand the language of animals. It was the snake which had given him this power.

One day, while passing a river, he heard some fishes crying out for help. They were trapped. He was a kind man and rescued them. The grateful fishes promised him their help whenever he should require it.

One day, the princess lost her ring in the river. The king announced that he would marry his daughter to anyone who recovered her ring. The servant took on the challenge and was about to jump into the river when three fishes popped out. They offered to recover the ring for him. The ring was recovered and the servant married the princess.

## 3 The Man and His Two Wives

A man had two wives. One wife was named Sarah while the other was called Clara. The two wives hated each other and were always fighting. Now, the husband was a middle-aged man and he had white as well as black hair.

One day, Clara decided that the black hair did not look good on him. She wanted to pluck out all the black hair. The man did not want to make his wife angry and allowed her to do so. So Clara plucked out all his grey hair. When Sarah saw her husband, she was shocked. His hair was all white! Now her husband looked really old. To make him look younger, she insisted on plucking out all the white hair on his head. The poor husband was now totally bald trying to please both his wives.

## 4 The Gnome

One day, a farmer saw a gnome on his fertile land. Thinking it to be a lucky sign, he asked the gnome if he had buried treasures somewhere in the field. The gnome nodded and replied, "Yes, precious jewels which you have never seen before."

The farmer said, "Since you have hidden it in my field I should get a share of it too." The cunning gnome said, "Only if you give me half of your harvest for two years. But I will take the top portion of the plant, while you will take the roots." The farmer realised that the gnome was tempted by the abundant grain crop that grew on his land. However, he agreed to the deal.

For the next two years, the clever farmer grew only potatoes in his field. So, for two years he took the potatoes while the gnome could only take the leaves of the potato plant. The clever farmer won and took all the treasures, while the gnome was left with nothing.

## 5 The Shroud

Once there lived a mother who loved her son more than anything else in the world. One day, after a grave illness, the boy died. His body was placed in a coffin covered with flowers and then buried.

The mother wailed all day and night for her dead son. At night she had a strange dream. Her child appeared before her and said, "Oh, Mother, the shroud of flowers is still wet because of your tears. Please do not weep and let it dry, for I need to sleep."

Startled by that strange dream, the mother made up her mind not to cry for her son anymore.

That night the child appeared in her dream with a lamp and gently said, "Mother, see how I'm resting in peace for your tears have dried."

## 6 King of the Golden Mountain

A fairy carried Heinel to a castle on a golden mountain. In the castle there lived a princess who had been turned into a snake by a wicked witch. The snake told Heinel, "I have been waiting for you. Please release me from the witch's spell." She told him that to free her he would have to undergo a lot of hardship. "Twelve men carrying steel chains will come every night to the castle. They will whip you. But you will have to bear it all without speaking a word for three nights." Heinel agreed to challenge the men. That night when the twelve men came Heinel stood silent. The second night the same was repeated. On the third night when Heinel killed all the twelve men, the snake was transformed into a beautiful maiden. She brought a magic potion and lovingly applied it to his injuries. Lo! All the pain vanished. Captivated by her beauty Heinel married her and was crowned king of the Golden Mountain.

# 7 The Three Brothers

A rich merchant had three sons. He wondered how to divide his huge mansion among his three sons, who wished to acquire his wealth upon his death. After much thought on the subject he came up with a plan.

One day, he called the three brothers and told them, "I will give my wealth to the person who can master a trade." The three brothers were happy with this condition and rushed to learn a job. The eldest became a blacksmith, the second a barber and the third a fencing master.

After each became skilled at their craft they returned home. Their father asked them to give proof of their skills.

The eldest stopped a horse-drawn carriage, took out the horseshoes and quickly made new ones. The father was impressed with his son's achievement. The eldest son thought he was the best and the deserved the property.

Then the merchant called his second son. He lifted a rabbit, lathered him up with soap and then shaved off his whiskers and fur with the skill of an expert barber. Seeing his father's happy face he thought that he would get the wealth.

When it was time to test his third son, the rains set in. Skillfully brandishing his sword above his head, the youngest son, stopped all the raindrops from pouring onto his body. The father, who had not seen anything like this before, was astonished. He immediately gave the entire property to his youngest son. The other two brothers stood stupefied; they agreed that this indeed was a masterpiece.

After the merchant's death all the sons lived happily in the huge mansion.

# 8 The New Hat

Pansy had a new hat made of freshly picked rose petals. She went for a walk wearing her new hat. She had gone just a few steps when she heard a flutter of wings and before she knew it her hat had disappeared. She looked up to see it in Sam Starling's beak. "Come back, Sam!" Pansy shouted. Sam dropped the hat and it fluttered to the ground right by the side of Tommy Tortoise. Rose petals were Tommy's favourite food.

"No! Don't eat my new hat, Tommy," said Pansy. "I'll find you something else." She found a dandelion. But the black bird got to it first. Pansy looked around and found some runner beans. But this time Peter the puppy came by and ran away with the beans. Sadly Pansy walked up to Toby, "I couldn't bring you any food Tommy, but please let me have my hat." For an answer, Pansy heard the soft snores of Tommy the Tortoise. She quietly picked up her hat and made her way home, feeling very happy.

## 9 Three Surgeons

Once there were three surgeons who thought they knew their job perfectly.

One day, they were travelling and came to an inn where they decided to spend the night. The innkeeper asked them who they were and challenged them to prove their skills. The surgeons decided to take out an organ each, and put it in again the next morning. The innkeeper was puzzled. Actually, the surgeons had special glue, which when rubbed, joined parts together. One surgeon cut off his hand, the other cut his eye, while another took his heart out. The innkeeper instructed his maid to kept the three organs in the cupboard.

At night, the maid unknowingly left the cupboard open while she was serving her husband dinner. A cat came and took the organs away. The maid was terrified and her husband hurriedly replaced the organs with a thief's hand, a pig's heart, and a cat's eye.

The next day, the surgeons fixed the organs in their bodies. They found that the man with the pig's heart only stuck to dirty places. The one with the thief's hand stole a man's purse and the one with the cat's eye constantly twitched his eyes. When they realised the mistake they went back to the inn and confronted the innkeeper. The maid saw them and fled. The surgeons angrily demanded money from the innkeeper who was so frightened that he gave them all he had.

The surgeons were very rich now but they knew that money could not replace what they had lost.

## 10 The Curious Farmer

Farmer John had a peculiar habit. He was always curious about what others were up to. Instead of tilling his own land, he wasted hours and hours prying into what the other farmers were doing.

John's master noticed this habit and was annoyed. One day, he decided to teach John a lesson.

That night, he invited John for dinner. He told him to eat whatever was served on the table, and specifically asked him not to open the lid of a bowl till he came back. John was very curious. While eating his food, John kept looking at the bowl from time to time. Unable to contain his curiosity anymore, he opened the lid, and out flew a bee and stung John's nose. He howled in pain.

The master, who was hiding himself to observe John, came out and said, "You see, curiosity kills the cat." John had learnt his lesson and cried out in pain, promising to mend his ways.

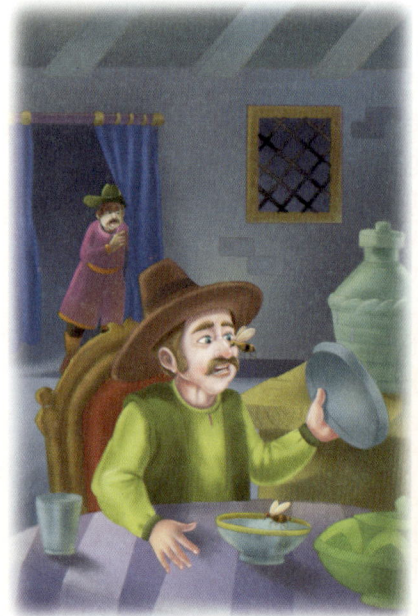

## 11 The Three Green Twigs

Long, long ago there lived a hermit who never sinned. God was very pleased with him.

One day, seeing a man being hanged, the hermit remarked, "The man is getting what he deserved."

God was displeased with the hermit for making such a remark. He declared that the hermit would have to repent till the time three green twigs appeared on a dry branch.

The repentant hermit was once explaining to three robbers how he was still atoning for one little mistake.

Listening to the hermit's story, the robbers realised their mistake too and begged for God's mercy. Just then, three twigs sprouted from the branch and everyone understood that to be the sign of forgiveness. They rejoiced for the hermit and vowed never to commit a crime again.

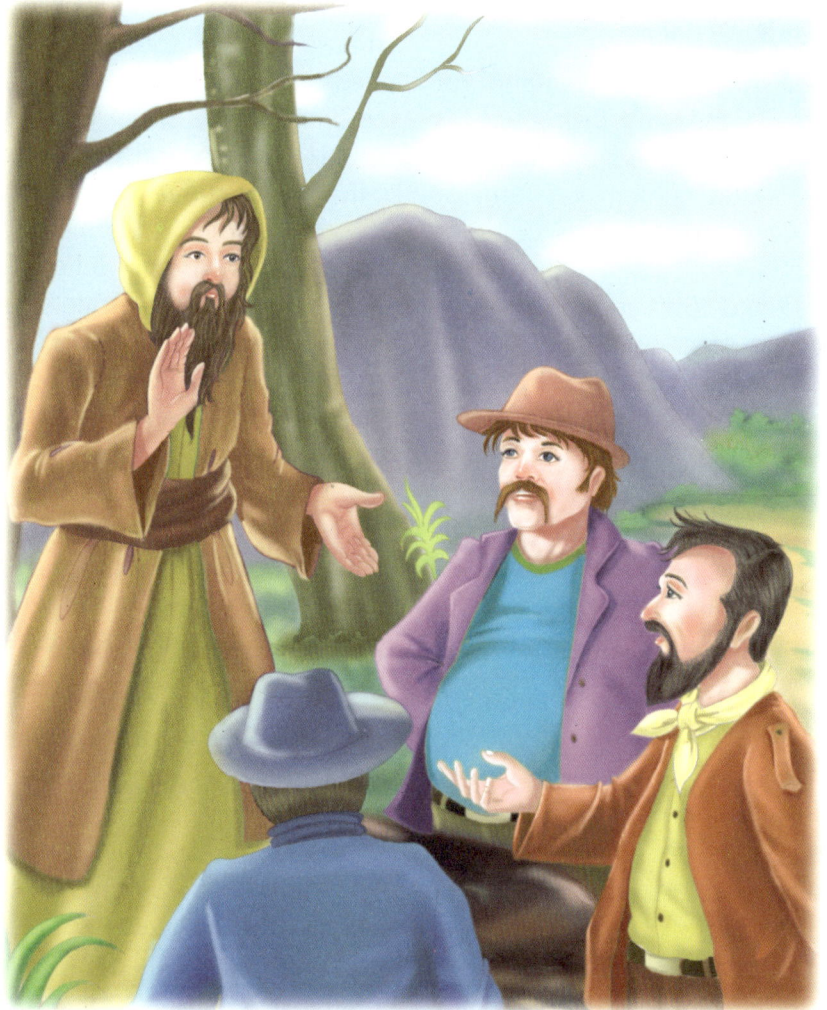

## 12 Philosophers Three

One day, a bear, a fox, and an opossum were walking together. Suddenly, it began to rain heavily and soon they were caught in a flood. There was water everywhere.

The bear wanted to show the fox and the opossum that he was not afraid of the flood and he went ahead to fight it. "Death comes easily to cowards but not to the brave one," he declared proudly. Although he tried hard to fight the mighty waters and keep himself afloat, he failed and almost drowned.

The fox laughed aloud and said, "Oh, you are foolish. I know a better trick to combat the flood." Then he went and hid in the hollow stump of a tree nearby.

The opossum said, "To challenge or confront the enemy that is stronger than us is foolhardy. It is sensible to know the nature of one's enemy and accordingly take action" Saying so, the opossum lay down and pretended to be dead!

## 13 Wise Folks

One day, before leaving for work, a peasant instructed his wife, "Take the three cows to the cattle dealer. Ask him for three hundred silver coins in exchange." The cattle dealer took two cows and promised to return later with the entire amount and take the third cow too. The wife agreed and gave the cattle dealer the cows. When the peasant returned, he was furious. "You fool! You deserve a good beating. But I will spare you if I find someone stupider than you," he exclaimed. The next day, he took a ride on a wagon. A foolish woman kept standing for the entire journey instead of sitting on her cattle or the pile of straw. He casually told the woman that he had come from heaven. Believing him, she promptly handed over her bag of coins and asked him to give it to her husband who lived there. Her son gave him a horse to journey to heaven.

Narrating his experience he told his wife, "If there are such fools on earth wise men will always win."

## 14 The Dog and the Ox

Once, a farmer had a very hardworking ox and a very lazy dog. While, the ox worked hard and ploughed the fields all day, the lazy dog would lie on the soft hay and sleep.

One day, the ox returned after working in the fields all day long. He was very tired and hungry. Alas! He was shocked to find that the dog was sleeping on his lunch.

When the ox tried to go near the hay to have his food, the lazy dog barked and chased him away. The ox was very angry and tried many times but the dog snarled at him ferociously. After trying many times, the ox finally had to give up.

Tired and hungry, the ox was very upset and went to the grassy banks of a brook and thought, "Those who are lazy do not let those who are hardworking enjoy their rewards either!"

# 15 The Snake Friend

Once there lived a snake and a little girl who were very fast friends. Every day when the mother served her daughter milk and bread, the snake popped out of its hole to share the food. But it only drank the milk. In return, the snake gave the little girl many lovely gifts.

One day, the girl didn't want to eat her food. When the snake arrived to share her food, the girl said, "You will get the milk but you have to eat the bread too." The snake refused to do so and the girl got angry. She hit him with a spoon on his head. Just then, her mother entered. "Snake! Snake!" she cried in fear. She was unaware of her daughter's friendship with the snake. Angrily, she picked up a log of wood lying nearby and threw it at the snake and killed it.

The little girl became very sad for she had lost her only true friend. She became pale and gave up drinking milk and eating bread.

# 16 Blue Light

Once many years ago, a soldier was wrongfully expelled from service by a king. Humiliated and disheartened, he left the kingdom and went away.

One day, he found a blue light, which actually belonged to a witch. He switched on the shining blue light to light his pipe. Whoosh! All of a sudden, a black dwarf emerged and said, "Command, master! I will fulfil all you wishes." At first the soldier was taken aback. Then a bright idea struck him.

Armed with the blue light he went back to the kingdom. "Bring me the princess and make her my slave!" he ordered the slave. Every night as instructed, the dwarf would fetch the princess and send her back in the morning.

The princess bore this for sometime and kept quiet. Finally, one day, she went to the king. The king was furious at hearing this. "Leave your shoes at the kidnapper's house, my child," he told his daughter. That night the king's guards went to search for the shoes. The dwarf could not make the shoes vanish, and the king's men captured the soldier. Unfortunately, the soldier forgot to bring the blue light with him. "Throw him in prison!" thundered the king.

The guards put the soldier in prison where he kept lamenting about his misfortune. As for the blue light, why it is still lying in the old cave where the soldier left it!

## 17 The Louse and the Flea

Once upon a time a little louse and a tiny flea lived together in a house. One day, the louse fell into an oven and was burnt to death. At this, the flea was devastated and began to cry loudly.

The kitchen door asked the flea why he was crying. "My friend, the little louse has burnt to death," replied the flea and wept and wept. Hearing this sad tale the door began to creak. Next to it was a broomstick, which asked the door why it was making such a noise. "The louse has died and the flea is crying," replied the door. On hearing this, the broom was also heartbroken and began sweeping the floor violently.

A cart, which was passing by, heard the commotion and asked the broom the reason for the chaos. Hearing the broom's tale, it wheeled rapidly across the fields. Seeing the cart dashing towards it, a pile of hay immediately stopped the cart. The cart narrated the entire story. Heartbroken, the haystack burst into flames.

Meanwhile, a tree standing next to the haystack also heard the story and shed its leaves in sorrow. Just then, a girl was passing by with a water pitcher and asked the tree what the matter was. It told her the sad tale. Shocked, the girl broke into tears. Her pitcher fell down and the water flowed into the river.

The river heard the water's tale and gushed so violently that the flea, the door, the broomstick, the cart, the haystack, the tree, the girl and the water pitcher all drowned in it.

## 18 Hans the Giant Caught in the Well

Hans was a kind giant. He used to work for a stingy farmer. When it was time to pay the giant for his services, the cunning farmer decided not to give him any money. The farmer's wife suggested that they kill the giant instead.

They thought of a plan and persuaded the giant to go to a well. As soon as the unsuspecting giant descended to the depths of the well, they lifted a huge grinding mortar and threw it on Hans's head. Thinking that the giant would die with the weight, they returned home happily. But the mortar was too small to harm Hans. It broke on his head and got stuck around his neck like a girdle. Hans quickly climbed out of the well and decided to go back to his master's house.

On seeing Hans return home with a stone collar around his neck, the farmer and his wife were very afraid. They begged for mercy, and handed their entire money and wealth to Hans.

## 19 The Miser

A miser once sold everything he had and bought gold instead.

He carefully buried the gold in a hole near his house. He used to look at the gold daily and admire it. One of his workmen noticed him doing this and one day, he dug the spot where the gold lay hidden and stole it.

The next day, when the miser found the hole empty he could not believe that someone had stolen all his gold. He cried loudly and began to tear his hair in despair.

On hearing the cause of his grief, his neighbour gave him a stone and advised, "Don't feel sad. Place this stone in the hole and imagine that it is the gold. It will make no difference since you did not make any use of the gold as long as you had it."

## 20 The Three Billy Goats Gruff

There lived three billy goats who decided to climb a mountain to chew grass. But a wooden bridge had to be crossed to reach the mountain. Underneath it lived a one-eyed troll (giant), who ate up all those who tried to cross the bridge.

The smallest Billy Goat Gruff, (for that was their name), went first. As he stepped on the bridge, the troll shouted, "Who goes there across my bridge?"

"I am the smallest Billy Goat Gruff," came the reply.

"I shall eat you up," roared the troll.

"Please wait, for a bigger goat is on its way," said the small Billy Goat Gruff. The greedy troll decided to let him go.

The second billy goat also told the troll the samething and crossed the bridge. On seeing the third billy goat, the troll pounced on him. But the goat was big and he knocked the troll down with his huge horns and killed it.

## 21 The Lion and the Statue

Once upon a time in ancient Greece, a man and a lion were arguing with each other. The man said, "I am stronger than you are!" The lion got angry and insisted, "No! Never! How dare you say this! I am stronger!" Then, the man showed the lion a statue of Hercules tearing a lion in two. The man said, "Look! I am stronger than you!" The clever lion replied, "A man made this statue. This is not how a lion would have made it! This sculptor did not ask this lion for his opinion before making the statue!" The man realised that the lion was speaking the truth. He said, "You are right. The reality is not always how we see it. Let us be friends!" The lion agreed and they became very good friends and never argued with each other again.

## 22 The Generous Brother

Evening, Midnight and Sunrise were three powerful brothers. One day, they set out to search for the king's missing daughters in the forest.

In the forest, the three brothers went out hunting. When Evening killed a sheep, a man beat him up for killing the animal. When his brothers enquired, Evening felt ashamed to tell the truth and said that he fell down. The next day when the man beat up Midnight, he too gave a similar reason for his injury. Finally, Sunrise beat up the man on the third day and mocked his brothers saying, "I have resolved the problem of your injuries."

When Sunrise rescued the missing girls from a cave, the king decided to honour him by crowning him the next king.

Thinking that Sunrise would not allow them to stay in the palace, Midnight and Evening decided to leave. However, Sunrise stopped them saying they would all stay together like a happy family.

# 23 The Water of Life

A king had three sons. Once when he fell ill, the sons were anxious to cure him. An old man told them, "Search for the water of life. It will cure the ailment."

The sons set out in search of the water. On their way, they met a dwarf. "Where are you going?" asked the dwarf. The first two princes went away without answering him. But the youngest prince told the dwarf that they were searching for the water of life. The dwarf instructed him, "Strike open the door of the castle ahead with this magic wand and feed the lions of the castle. You will find what you seek. Henceforth you shall wipe out all wars and all famines with this magic wand. But beware of your brothers for they shall harm you." The prince did as he was told and found the cup of water.

The prince met his brothers and told them about the water of life. They came across a kingdom plagued with war and famine. The prince waved his magic wand and peace returned to the kingdom at once. The brothers were jealous and at night, when the prince fell asleep they exchanged the water with some seawater.

Then they took the water of life to their father and his condition improved. They also influenced him to believe that the youngest prince had planned to kill his father. He was thrown out of the country.

One day, the people of the peaceful kingdom came searching for the prince to thank him. When the king heard the truth, he wept for his mistake. He sent out armies to search for his son and soon was reunited. He banished the older brothers.

# 24 The Devil's Grandmother

One day, a devil found three men being chased by the king's army. "Please save us," implored the three men. The devil agreed. "But you have to serve me for seven years. At the end you must solve a puzzle."

The men readily agreed and the devil rescued them. As the seven years neared its end they grew anxious. They met an old woman who suggested, "Go to the monster's grandmother. She may help you."

The grandmother took pity on the men. She hid them in a room. When the monster came to visit she asked him to unravel the puzzle. The devil said, "In the great North Sea lies a dead dog-fish; that shall be your roast meat, and the rib of a whale shall be your silver spoon, and a hollow old horse's hoof shall be your wine glass."

The men memorised the answer and repeated it to the devil when he arrived after seven years. The devil lost his power and ran away.

## 25 The Owl

One day a huge horned owl lost her way. Fearing attacks from other birds, she took shelter in a granary next to an old house. The keeper of the granary saw the bird perched on the roof and yelled for help. He ran to his master and told him about the owl.

The master came armed with an axe but when he saw the huge bird he too was terrified and fled. A village council was set up and there it was decided that every villager would arm himself with weapons and attack the bird.

However, when the villagers arrived, they saw the bird and all their bravery disappeared. Then one brave man stepped out, took a spear and sword and climbed up the roof. He had nearly reached when the bird flapped his wings, snapped its beak, and gave such a loud shriek that the man fainted and fell to the ground below.

Unable to find any other alternative, they burnt the granary and killed the bird.

## 26 The Sportsman and the Squirrel

Once a sportsman had injured a squirrel, which was now trying hard to drag itself away from there. The sportsman took pity on it and thought of ending the squirrel's misery. So he ran after it with a stick.

The squirrel, who was already in pain, soon felt tired and said to the sportsman, "I don't wish to doubt your sense of compassion though it has come too late. But I wish that you were a little observant so that you could see that right now my greatest wish is to be left alone as I am in this painful situation."

The sportsman felt very ashamed and guilty on hearing the squirrel's words. He realised that he had no right to kill anyone even if he thought that it was for their own good. Then the sportsman apologised to the squirrel and hung his head and walked away in shame.

# 27 The Fox and the Horse

Once upon a time a peasant had a faithful horse. When the horse grew old, the peasant decided to drive out the frail animal. He ordered the old horse to return only if he managed to get a lion.

The horse was very sad and left his master's house. On the way, the horse met a kind fox and told him his story. The fox asked him to follow his instructions.

He asked the horse to pretend to be dead. Meanwhile, he went and invited a lion to eat the horse. The fox suggested that the lion should rather drag the horse to his cave and enjoy his meal there. Then the clever fox asked the lion to turn around so that he could tie the horse to his tail. However, as soon as the lion turned to do so, the fox immediately tied the lion's feet to the horse's tail.

The horse galloped away with the lion tied to his tail. When he reached home, his master was very pleased and kept him in service again.

# 28 Androcles and the Lion

Androcles was a Roman slave who escaped from his oppressive master and started living in the jungles. There, he saw an injured lion with a thorn stuck in his paw. Kind Androcles plucked out the thorn and put the lion out of pain. They lived together until the emperor's men found Androcles and took him back. As a punishment for fleeing, Androcles was thrown inside a ring to be eaten up by lions. Lots of people, including the emperor gathered to watch this spectacle. The lion came. But instead of eating him up, it stroked and caressed Androcles. It was the same lion that he had helped in the forest! Shocked at this strange behaviour, the emperor demanded an explanation. When Androcles explained what had happened, he was pardoned and the lion was set free.

## 29 The Lazy Spinner

A spinner had a very lazy wife. Instead of completing her work, she often left the materials all entangled on the spinning wheel. When her husband scolded her for the mess, she fought with him.

She tried various tricks so that she didn't have to work but failed every time. One day, she had an idea and decided to settle the score once and for all.

Now, fresh yarn, when boiled for too long, can lose its firmness and break into threads. To deceive her husband, she gathered some threads and put them for boiling. Then she instructed her husband to take care of the yarn for if it boils for too long, it will turn into fibre. Then she pretended that she had urgent work and left.

After some time the man came to see the yarn, but he found threads instead. He thought it was due to his neglect that the yarn had been spoilt and swore not to ever spin again.

## 30 The Monkey and the Dolphin

Once took a monkey accompanied a sailor on a sea journey. A violent storm arose off the coast of Greece and everyone had to swim for their lives.

A dolphin saw the monkey and thought him to be a man. It carried him to the shore. When they arrived near the coast of Athens, the dolphin asked the monkey if he was an Athenian. The monkey replied that he was the crowned prince of Athens who would soon become the king. Then the dolphin asked the monkey if he visited Piraeus, which was the most famous harbour of Athens, often.

The foolish monkey thought that Piraeus was a man and replied that he knew him very well as he was his best friend. The monkey's lies angered the dolphin and he took the monkey down into the water and drowned him.

# 31 The Dog and the Sparrow

A dog left his master's house after being forced to starve for several days. On the way, he met a kind sparrow who offered him food and shelter. They became good friends and the sparrow risked his life to steal pieces of meat and bread for the dog. Finally, the dog wanted some rest and slept on one side of the road, while the sparrow kept a vigil over his friend.

A while later, a driver came down the road pulling his horse-drawn wagon and demanded that the dog be removed. The sparrow refused to wake his friend and asked the driver to take another route. Angry, the driver wheeled his wagon over the dog's body and killed him.

The sparrow was grief-stricken. He leaked the barrels of wine in the wagon and pecked out the horse's eyes. In anger, the driver lashed his whip at the sparrow and it flew away.

When the driver reached home, his wife dragged him to the rooftop and showed him thousands of birds, which were pecking at their corn. In their midst was the sparrow, who was laughing, seeing the mess. "What sorrow has struck me," cried out the man. "Not yet," replied the sparrow.

Mad with anger, the man caught the sparrow and put it in his mouth. The sparrow struggled and screamed, "This will cost you your life." The man's wife grabbed a knife and struck at the sparrow. The sparrow escaped in time and the man was killed instead.

# Contents

*The Story of the Month:   Sleeping Beauty*

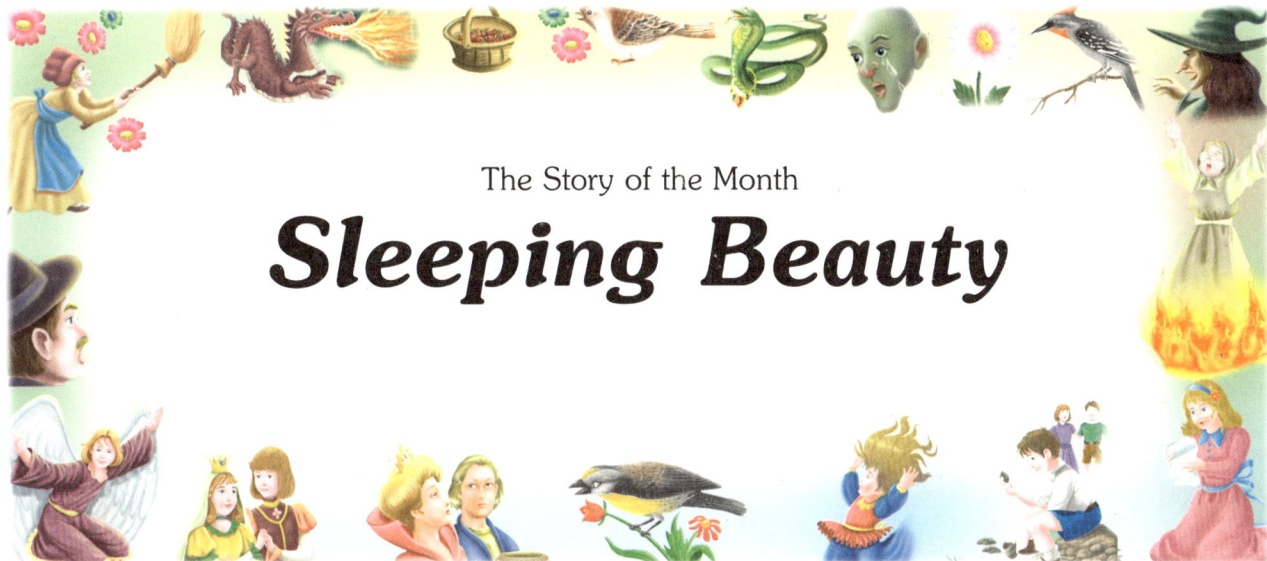

The Story of the Month

# Sleeping Beauty

# Sleeping Beauty

Once upon a time there lived a good king and his queen. They had no children for many years and were very sad.

Then one day, the queen gave birth to a lovely baby girl and the whole kingdom was happy. There was a grand celebration and all the fairies in the kingdom were invited. But the king forgot to invite an old fairy. She came to the celebrations but was very angry. Soon it was time to gift the baby with special wishes. The good fairies wished her well and said, "May she grow to be the most beautiful girl in the world! She will sing sweetly and dance so well!

She will live happily!" All the fairies blessed the baby and gave her beautiful gifts.

When it was the old fairy's turn, she said, "When the baby is sixteen she will touch a spindle, and die!" The king and queen were shocked and begged the fairy to forgive them and take her words back but the fairy refused to do so. When the other fairies saw the king and queen crying, they said, "We cannot undo what the old fairy has spoken. But we certainly can make it different. Your child shall not die when she touches the spindle. But she will fall into a deep sleep for a hun-

dred years. Then, a prince will come along and wake her up." Hearing this, the king and the queen were relieved. The king forbade everyone from spinning so that the princess would never touch a spindle.

The princess grew up to be a kind girl and helped people in need. Everybody loved her. Years passed. When the princess was sixteen years old, she was walking in the woods when she saw an old lady spinning. "What is this? May I try?" she asked The old lady said, "Of course, my pretty little child!" And the

princess sat down to spin. But the moment she touched the spindle, she fell to the floor in a deep slumber. The old lady took her back to the palace and the king and queen laid her on her bed and tucked her in. They were very sad and called the good fairies. The fairies felt sorry for them and cast a spell over the whole kingdom so that when the princess woke up after a hundred years, she would not be alone in the palace. Everyone, including the guards and the servants and the animals were now fast asleep. For a hundred years, they all slept soundly.

A hundred years passed. There came a prince from a far off land. He, along with his servants, went deep into the forest and crossed many rivers. Once the prince lost his way and was separated from the rest of the travellers. He came to the sleeping kingdom and was amazed. The guards, the servants, the cats and the cows were all fast asleep and snoring.

The prince reached the palace and entered it. No one moved. The prince then found the sleeping princess. She was such a beautiful girl that the prince kissed her. By that time, a hundred years had passed by and everyone was waking up, one by one. The princess yawned and opened her eyes. She saw the prince and smiled. She asked him "Are you my prince?" He was happy to hear her speak. The prince and the princess fell in love with each other. The prince wanted to marry the princess so they went to ask for permission from their parents.

The king and the queen arranged for a royal wedding. All the clothes the bride wore were a hundred years old, but she looked beautiful. Soon, they were married and then they rode away to the prince's kingdom far, far away.

## 1 The Pig Keeper

Once upon a time there lived a prince who loved a princess and wished to marry her.

One day, he sent her two beautiful gifts, a rose and a nightingale, asking her to marry him. Everybody loved the gifts but the princess was very haughty and said, "What useless gifts! This is not a silver rose or a mechanical nightingale! I will not accept these gifts." The prince tried to woo her and did all he could to persuade her to marry him but the haughty princess refused to change her mind. To teach her a lesson, the prince disguised himself as a pig keeper and took up a job in the royal sty. Whenever he was free, he made lovely little things for the princess.

One day, he made a pot with little bells on it, which tinkled when boiled water. The princess was enchanted by the pot and wanted it. The pig keeper agreed to give it to her on the condition that she would kiss him in exchange. The princess agreed. But just as the she was about the kiss the pig keeper, the king saw them and was very angry. The pig keeper then revealed that he was actually a prince. The princess was excited and wanted to marry him now but the prince refused and said to the king, "Sire, your daughter does not appreciate the real beauty of nature. She refused to marry me when I was a prince and gave her a rose and a nightingale. Instead, she liked a pot that tinkles and was willing to kiss a pig keeper for it! She should be happy with the tinkling pot and stay unmarried!"

## 2 The White and the Black Bride

A woman, her daughter and her stepdaughter were cutting fodder. God decided to test them and came in the form of an old man. He asked them the way. The woman and her daughter refused to help but the stepdaughter helped him. God cursed the woman and her daughter to become as dark as night. He made the stepdaughter as fair as day.

The fair maiden's brother, Reginer, was a coachman. He painted her picture on his coach. One day, the king saw her picture and wished to marry her. When the dark woman and her daughter heard this, they became jealous and pushed the fair maiden in a river where she turned into a swan.

One day, the swan was swimming in the river by the palace. As soon as she reached the palace, she was transformed back into the fair maiden. She told the king everything. The king married her and punished the mother and daughter.

# 3 The Nurse and the Wolf

Once upon a time there lived a wolf. One day, he was very hungry and began to prowl in a village nearby. He hoped to lay his hands on a piece of meat.

After a while, he came upon a nurse who was scolding a little child. She was saying, "If you don't stop crying this instant, I will feed you to the wolves! Stop crying now!" But the child did not listen to her and kept on crying. Now, this wolf was very foolish and he thought that the nurse really meant what she said and was going to give away the child. The hungry wolf waited and waited. But the nurse did not throw away the crying child. After a long time, the child stopped crying and the nurse took him home. Finally, the foolish wolf walked away, hungry and bitter.

# 4 Lazy Harry

Harry was an unhappy shepherd. He always grumbled that he had to take his goat for grazing. He decided to marry Trina, his neighbour, who also had a goat, so that she would take both the goats to graze together.

But Trina was also just as lazy as Harry. After they got married, she decided to exchange their goats with their neighbour for his beehive. Harry agreed and after that, they slept all day, as bees don't need to be taken care of.

One day Harry complained, "Trina, you eat away all the honey, so we will exchange the beehive for a goose that would lay eggs." Trina agreed and said, "We will have a child who would take care of the goose and sell the eggs." Harry said, "What if our child doesn't listen to us?" Trina said, "I will hit him like this." And she took a stick and waved it in the air.

Alas! It struck the pitcher of honey, which broke and all the honey spilled out.

## 5 The Dragon with a Hundred Heads

Once upon a time a brave knight was riding through the forest and there he met a dragon. This huge beast had hundred heads and spat fire. The knight, who had killed many beasts, was now afraid. "I will not be able to kill this beast!" he thought and ran away. After a while, when he rode deeper and deeper into the forest, he saw another dragon with one head but it had swift legs. "I can easily kill this one-headed monster!" he thought. He tried to kill it, but the beast was too quick and attacked him.

The dragon almost killed the brave knight. The knight thought, "I could have easily killed the beast with hundred heads by entangling all its heads together! I should never judge anything by its looks!"

## 6 Choosing a Bride

A young man wanted to get married. He knew three sisters who were equally beautiful and wanted to marry one of them. But he couldn't decide whom to choose for a wife. "Mother, who do you think will be the most suitable?" he asked his mother. His mother thought for a while, "You must invite the three sisters to dinner tomorrow."

The next day, the sisters were invited to dinner and cheese was served to them. The first one ate the cheese without removing the peel. The second one removed the peel so hastily that a lot of cheese was left on it and she wasted a lot of cheese with the peel. The third sister carefully peeled the cheese and then ate it so that none was wasted.

The mother silently observed what all the three sisters were doing and finally said to her son, "Marry the third sister, as she would run the household well." The young man married the third sister and lived very happily with her

## 7 George and Georgette

Once upon a time there lived two young people named George and Georgette. They both loved each other dearly and were engaged to be married soon.

One day, both George and Georgette went to the nearby woods for a walk. As they walked further and further, they heard the twitter of many birds. George heard the song of a thrush and turned to Georgette to show her the bird. But to his surprise, he found a thrush perched on a plant where Georgette once stood! George realised that the wicked witch of the woods had turned his beloved into a bird. He sat and cried bitterly, and then tired and hungry, he finally went off to sleep.

In his dream, he saw a red flower with a pearl in the centre. When George woke up, he went in search of this flower that he had seen in his dream. He knew it was magical. George found this red flower deep in the valley. There was a dewdrop settled in the centre of the flower. He went to the witch's house with the flower. He saw many cages with all sorts of birds. He knew these birds were all young girls that the witch had captured. How would he find Georgette among these birds? The witch spotted him. Quickly, George touched her with the magical flower. The witch was reduced to ashes at once and all the birds turned into lovely young girls.

Georgette ran to George and now they both were very happy. The king heard how brave George was and rewarded him with many gifts. The couple then got married and they lived happily ever after.

## 8 The Ear of Corn

Long, long ago, when God lived on the earth, the soil was very fertile. The stalk of a corn would bear hundreds of ears. But when anyone gets something in plenty, he takes it for granted.

One day, a woman was walking with her daughter along a cornfield. Suddenly, the daughter fell in a puddle and her frock got dirty. Without thinking, the woman quickly tore many beautiful ears of corn to clean her daughter's frock. When she had cleaned the frock, she carelessly threw the ears of corn on the roadside and walked away.

When God saw her do this, he was very angry and wanted to teach the people a lesson. He declared that corn would no longer have ears. When people heard about the curse, they begged God to leave something on the stalk at least for the chicken that would starve without corn. God took pity on the chicken and left fifty or sixty ears on the corn.

## 9 The Donkey Who Was a Prince

Once upon a time there lived a king and a queen. They were very unhappy because they did not have any children.

After many years, the queen gave birth to a baby but alas! It was a donkey. Nevertheless, the king and the queen loved the donkey and treated him like a little child. The donkey grew up in the palace like a prince. He was very fond of music and learnt to play the lute. One day, he looked at the mirror and saw his face in it. On seeing his real self, he was so sad that he decided to leave the palace and go away.

The donkey wandered around for a few days and reached another kingdom. He went to the palace and played his lute for the king. The king grew very fond of him and the donkey started living in the palace.

One day, the king decided to marry his daughter to the donkey. At first the princess refused but she gave in to her father's wishes. After the marriage, the princess seemed to be very happy. The king was surprised and wondered what was the reason. One evening he hid himself in his daughter's room.

At night, when the donkey came to the room, the king saw the donkey shed his skin and turn into a handsome prince. The king was speechless. Next morning, the donkey put his skin back again. The king made a plan and went to his daughter's room again the next day. At night, when the donkey removed his skin, the king took it away and burnt it.

After that, the prince never turned into a donkey again and the prince and princess lived happily ever after.

## 10 The Crows and the Serpent

Once a crow couple built their nest on a tree. But as luck would have it, there lived a serpent in a hole at the bottom of the same tree. When the crows were away, the serpent used to climb up the tree and eat the eggs. When the crows realised what was happening, they didn't know what to do to punish the serpent.

One day, the crows went to their friend, a jackal to ask him to help them get rid of the serpent. The jackal was very clever and made a plan. He asked the father crow to go to the king's palace and steal the queen's necklace.

The crow went to the palace and picked up the queen's necklace while she was bathing. Then he flew back and dropped the necklace in the serpent's hole. When the queen discovered that her necklace was missing, the king sent his guards to look for it. The guards found it in the serpent's hole and killed it. The crows were very happy and lived happily ever after.

# 11 The Rose

Once a poor woman had two little girls. The youngest child went to the woods every day to collect wood for the house.

One day, a strange little child helped her collect the wood and carry it home and then disappeared. The little girl told her mother about this strange child in the forest but her mother didn't believe her and thought that she was telling a tale.

One day, the girl came home and showed her mother a rose and said that the little child had given it to her and told her that when it was in full bloom, the child would come back. The mother put the rose in water.

Many days passed and one morning, the mother found her little girl lying dead but looking very happy.

The next morning the rose was in full bloom.

# 12 The Hazel Branch

One afternoon, a mother put her little baby to sleep. Then she decided to go to the woods to collect strawberries for her. After searching for a while, she found a bush with the reddest of strawberries. They were very sweet and juicy. Unfortunately, she did not see the venomous snake hiding there. As she bent to pick up the strawberries, the snake raised its head. She was very afraid and ran fast, but the snake followed her.

Finally, she came to a hazel bush. She decided to hide behind the bush until the snake was gone. When the snake had left, she came out and collected the strawberries. Then she looked gratefully at the hazel bush and said, "The hazel bush has protected me today, so it will protect others in the future too," and left to go home.

From that day onwards, a green hazel branch has become the surest protection against snakes and other creeping creatures.

# 13 The Sole

The kingdom of fishes was always in disorder. Fishes would swim in whichever direction they wanted. Some tried to go between those who wanted to swim together, and some got in the other's way and there was chaos all around.

Finally, one wise fish said, "We must choose a king who will maintain peace and order in the kingdom." Let's have a race and the one who swims the fastest would be declared the king." The pike, the herring, the carp, the perch and even the sole participated in the race.

As soon as the race began, the herring darted like an arrow and came first. The other fishes shouted, "The herring is first."

Meanwhile, the sole, who had lagged far behind, was jealous of the herring and started shouting, "The naked herring, the naked herring." From that day onwards, the sole fish has a mouth on one side as a punishment for taunting the herring.

# 14 The Boys and the Giant

Once three boys were playing near the forest. Suddenly, a giant came out. He wanted to eat the boys for dinner. So he caught them and put them in his bag. He was very happy as he walked back home. One of the boys had a knife in his pocket with which he cut a little hole in the bag. One by one, the three boys slipped out. When the giant reached his cave, he called his brother, "Come, I have brought food." But when he opened his bag, the boys were not in it.

Meanwhile, the boys reached the village and told the elders about the giants. The villagers took bows and arrows with them and followed the boys to the cave. The two giants were sleeping at that time. The angry villagers started shooting arrows and soon killed the giants. The villagers praised the three boys for their bravery.

## 15 Mary Ann and the Front Door

Mary Ann often forgot to close the front door when she went out of the house. Every day she would take lunch for her husband, Joseph, who worked in the fields. Knowing his wife and her annoying habit, always reminded her, "Don't forget the door." But poor Mary Ann was very forgetful.

One day, as she was going to take food for her husband, Mary Ann had an idea. The best way not to forget the door was to take it with her.

So she took the door off its hinges and put it on her back. "Now that I am carrying the door, who will carry the lunch? " she wondered. Then she hung the lunch basket on the handle of the door and said, "Let the door carry the lunch, not me!" and left for the fields. On the way, some thieves saw Mary Ann carrying the door. They understood what had happened and rushed to her house and saw the front door missing. They entered and stole everything that was there!

## 16 Why the Sky Is So High

Long ago, the sky was very low. It was so low that people could touch it if they raised their hands. At the horizon, where the sky nearly touched the earth, was a village. Here lived an old woman all by herself. All day long she was busy with her household chores. Cleaning her utensils, scrubbing the floor, and dusting her courtyard.

One day, she saw that her courtyard was very dirty. So she picked up her broomstick to clean it. She swept the ground so fast and so hard that it raised a storm of dust. In a minute, her house and the entire village became covered with dust and when it reached the sky, it started coughing. The poor sky nearly choked as the woman continued sweeping the ground. .Suddenly the sky sneezed. It was such a thunderous sneeze that the whole village shook! People ran helter-skelter, scared that the sky might fall. But the old woman kept sweeping oblivious of what was happening.

After a while, it became so unbearable for the sky that he started crying helplessly. Huge teardrops fell on the earth. It made the courtyard muddy. Now this was too much for the woman to bear. She raised her broomstick and whacked the sky, "Get lost you wet blanket!" she yelled. The sky was so scared that he moved higher and higher and swore never to come down again.

## 17 The Daisy and the Lark

Once there was a little daisy that grew outside a garden. The proud flowers of the garden looked down upon the daisy as nobody could see her there. But the daisy was very happy bathing in the sun.

One day, a lark came and sat on a tree. The peonies, who were very large, and the tulips, who were brightly coloured, thought that the lark would sing to them. But the lark liked the daisy's golden centre and her silver white petals. So he came down to where the daisy was and sang sweetly to her. The other flowers of the garden started envying the little daisy.

The next day, the daisy heard the song of the lark, but this time it was a sad song. Some naughty boys had caught the lark and put him in a cage. She wished that she could help the lark but what could a little flower do.

Meanwhile, the boys came and began pulling the grass around her, they said, "This grass would be good for the lark." They took a little piece of earth with the grass and the daisy on it and put it in the cage.

The daisy was happy to be with the lark who was weeping bitterly, "They have given me a little grass in exchange of the whole world," he complained. The daisy tried to console the lark but the lark just wept and wept.

Soon, the daisy was thirsty and told the lark, "They have left without giving me water."

The night passed and in the morning when the boys came to see the lark, they saw that it was dead while the daisy had withered.

## 18 The Two Bears in the Sky

There once lived a good giant in a village. He was hard-working and did the work of a dozen people. He used to help the villagers in their work. One day two bears, one male and one female, came to the village.

The people were frightened and ran to the giant for help. The giant ran to the place where the bears were frightening an old woman. The giant caught hold of the male bear and hurled him into the sky and he was suspended there. He did the same to the female bear, but being lighter, she went higher up than the male bear. The bears were separated from each other

The female bear called out to the male bear, "Come here!" The male bear replied, "No, you come here."

Ever since, the two bears have been arguing as to who will go to whom. When you look up into the night sky you can still see two constellations, "The Great Bear" and "The Little Bear."

# 19 The Star Money

Once there was a girl whose father and mother had died. She had no home to live. All she had were the clothes she was wearing and a piece of bread.

One day, she decided to go to the country. While she was walking down, she met an old man who asked her for food. She was a kind girl and without thinking of what she would eat, she gave her bread away. As she moved further, she found a little child shivering with cold. She took pity and gave away her frock to the little child. As she stood in the dark of the night, hungry and shivering in the cold, a few stars fell from the sky. She was surprised to see they were silver coins. She looked down to find herself wearing a pretty dress of the finest linen. She took the coins and was never poor again.

# 20 The Swan and the Goose

Once a rich man bought a swan and a goose. He put them both in the pond in his garden. The swan was bought to enhance the beauty of the pond but the goose was to be cooked and eaten. Soon, the two birds became close friends and were inseparable.

One day, there was a party at the house and the rich man ordered the cook to slaughter the goose and cook it for dinner. The cook obediently went out to fetch the goose. But the cook was drunk and caught the swan by mistake. He held it tightly in his hands and as he was about to raise the knife to cut the swan's throat and kill it, the swan began to sing. The cook was taken aback.

It is said that a swan sings a beautiful song when it is about to die. When the cook heard the swan's beautiful and melodious song he took pity on it and spared its life.

This shows that one can get out of a bad situation by making proper use of words as the swan did.

## 21 The Moon Cake

Once a cunning man saw a boy with a cake. He wanted to eat it and decided to play a trick on the little boy to take the cake away from him. He went to the boy and said, "Give the cake to me; I can make it look like the moon." The boy was delighted with the idea and gave it to him. The man took a bite and the cake looked like a crescent moon.

Now the boy was not happy, so the man took another bite and made it into a half moon.

The boy still complained that the moon was small.

The clever man said, "I can make it like a full moon, but the full moon can only appear after the old moon disappears." He ate the whole cake and ran away, while the boy waited for the new moon to appear.

## 22 The Lonely Tree

The short tree was sad and lonely. All the other trees around her were tall and elegant. They had many visitors like, chirpy sparrows and fuzzy squirrels. No one visited the short tree. She longed for a friend. One day, she heard an unmelodious tone. She looked around and found a woodpecker singing blissfully. "Will you stop singing?" she asked the woodpecker. "I entertain everybody with my sweet voice, and you are asking me not to sing," the woodpecker shot back. "You have an appalling voice," said the tree. The woodpecker was shocked! Nobody had ever told him that. Tears welled up in his eyes as he explained, "I am a lonely woodpecker and I thought if I entertain people they would be my friend." The short tree felt sorry. "Will you be my friend?" she asked. "Sure!" said the woodpecker, "but you have to let me stay on your short branch." "And you have to stop singing!" said the short tree. The two became great friends and lived happily ever after.

## 23 The Duration of Life

When God created the world, he decided to fix the duration of life for all creatures. He called the donkey and said, "Will thirty years be fine for you?" The donkey replied, "I will have to carry heavy burden, thirty years is too long." God reduced his age to eighteen years. Then he called the dog and said, "I hope thirty years is fine for you." The dog said, "I will soon lose my teeth and sit in the corner, thirty years is too much." God reduced it to twelve years. Then came the monkey and God said, "How does thirty years sound?" The monkey replied, "I have to do silly things to make people laugh. Thirty years is too much." God reduced it to ten years.

Then God called man and asked him if thirty years was good enough for him to live well. The man replied, "I have to build my house and plant the trees. How can I die before I get pleasure from my house and before the plants start bearing fruits? Thirty years is too less." God said, "I will give you eighteen years of the donkey's life."

The man was greedy and wanted more. God said, "You can take twelve years of the dog's life." "Can I have some more?" asked the man. Finally God said, "Take ten years of the monkey's life and no more."

Therefore, the first thirty years of man's life are his own, when he enjoys. The next eighteen are of a donkey's when he has to carry burdens. The next ten years are those of a dog's life when he loses his teeth and lies in a corner, and the last ten years are that of monkey's life when he does silly things!

## 24 St. Joseph in the Forest

Once there lived two sisters. The elder sister was very clever and wicked while the younger one was good and kind at heart.

One morning, the younger sister went to the forest to pick berries. In the evening, she lost her way and reached a small hut where she met an old man. He was St. Joseph. She made soup for him and gave him more than her share. He then asked her to sleep in the bed while he slept on the floor. But she said that the ground was good enough for her and let him sleep on the bed. In the morning, the girl found a bag of gold kept for her along with a letter saying, 'This is for the girl who slept on the straw."

When the elder sister saw the bag she was jealous and wanted to get the gold, so she went to St. Joseph's hut. She was hungry so made soup but she gave him none and ate it all. At night she refused to sleep on the floor. She bitterly returned home the next morning without any gold.

## 25 The Old Man Made Young Again

Once upon a time when God lived on earth, he went with St. Peter to an ironsmith's house. Along came a beggar who was crippled and old.

St. Peter asked God to make the beggar a young man. God agreed to do so. He put the old beggar on the ironsmith's coals and then immersed him in some water.

The beggar now came out as a young man. The ironsmith's mother-in-law saw all this. She was very greedy and asked the beggar if the coals were very hot. The beggar replied, "No, they were as cold as dew." When God had left, the ironsmith asked his mother-in-law if she would like to be young again. She said yes and he put her on the burning coals. She cried out in pain and howled and the ironsmith's wife came running.

When she saw her mother all burnt and injured, she was very angry at her mother's greed in wanting to be young again and her husband's foolishness.

## 26 The Sea Hare

Once there was a princess who had twelve windows in her castle from which she could see her whole kingdom. She didn't really want to get married. One day, she declared that she would only marry the man who could hide from her.

Many young men tried to hide somewhere in the kingdom, but the princess saw them from the windows and had them beheaded.

There was a young man who saved a fox's life. The fox promised to help him hide from the princess. It took him to a magical pool where the young man took a dip and became a small sea hare. The sea hare hid in the princess's hair. When the princess looked out of her windows, she could not see him. When she gave up, the sea hare went back to the pool and changed into his real form. The princess had no choice but to marry him.

## 27 The Pride of Icarus

The king of Crete had imprisoned an inventor named Daedalus, and his son, Icarus, in a castle with high walls so that they could not escape. But Daedalus had an idea by which they could escape.

He made a pair of wings, which he stuck on his shoulders with wax. Then he made another pair for his son. The father and son moved their arms up and down and flapped their wings. Soon they took off and rose above the walls. On reaching Greece, Daedalus landed on the ground and asked Icarus to come down too. But Icarus was enjoying himself up in the air and was very proud that he could fly like a bird.

His father kept calling out to Icarus to come down but Icarus was enjoying himself and kept flying higher and higher until the heat from the sun melted the wax that joined the wings to his shoulders.

The wings broke off and poor Icarus couldn't fly anymore and fell down and died.

## 28 Adrian and the Magic Stone

Once there lived a boy named Adrian. He was so silly that his friends always made fun of him. One day, his friends came to Adrian's house and said, "Hurry up, Adrian! We must go to the riverbank right now! There is a black magic stone that we need to find!" Adrian asked them why. They said, "The person who finds this stone will get magical powers. He will become invisible!" Adrian raced to the riverbank and began collecting all the black-coloured stones. After sometime, his friends who were fooling him began to say, "Oh! It looks like Adrian found the stone! We can't find him! He is invisible!" Saying this, they began throwing stones at him, pretending that they couldn't see him. Foolish Adrian believed them and did not say anything to them.

# 29 The Three Sluggards

The king of Lazyland had three sons. He loved them equally and didn't know whom to make his heir.

When he was on his deathbed he called his sons and said to them, "Whoever is the laziest, will be the king." The first one said, "Then make me the king for I am so lazy that if I am lying down and something were to get into my eyes I would not take it out because I have to sleep."

The second son said, "No, I should be made the king for I am so lazy that if I am lying near the fireplace and the fire is burning my feet, I would not move them aside."

The third son said, "I am so lazy that if I were being hanged and the rope was already around my neck and somebody gave me a knife, I would rather be hanged than take the trouble of cutting the rope with the knife." The king realised that the third son was the laziest since he was willing to die so easily and made him the king.

# 30 Joy and Sorrow

A tailor used to quarrel with his wife. One day, she complained to the king. The tailor was arrested and jailed. He promised never to beat his wife again and to share all his joys and sorrows with her. The king set him free but soon the tailor returned to his old ways. He quarrelled with his wife and threw things at her. When the things hit his wife, he laughed, but when they missed her, he yelled.

Soon, he was arrested again and brought in front of the king, who said, "You promised not to beat your wife and share all your sorrows and joys with her." The tailor replied, "I didn't beat her. I threw things at her. If they hit her I was joyful and she was sorrowful but when they missed her, she was joyous and I was sorry." The king was amused at the tailor's reply but he punished him anyway.

# 31 The Sparrow Chicks

Once a sparrow lived in a nest with four chicks. One day, some boys destroyed their nest but the little sparrows managed to fly away to safety. The sparrow was sad that his children were separated from each other and was afraid because the chicks were gone before he could warn them of the dangers of the world and how to deal with them.

After a few months, in the autumn, when all the sparrows gathered together for their yearly meeting, he found his chicks in a wheat field. They were all overjoyed to meet each other and be united again. The sparrow asked his children how they had spent the summer.

The first sparrow said that he had stayed in a garden and ate caterpillars and worms. The second one said that he had lived in a royal court, and the third one had spent the summer on the highway. All the three sparrows had learnt about the dangers of the world and how to protect themselves.

The fourth one was the weakest of all the four sparrows. The father asked him to stay with him so that he could protect him against the eagles and hawks. Then the father asked him where he had spent his summer. The little chick replied that he had spent his summer in a church and had learnt that he who commits himself to God need not protect himself for God will be his protector.

The father realised that his fourth son too had learnt everything and would be safe.

# Contents

*The Story of the Month:   Puss in Boots*

The Story of the Month

# Puss in Boots

# Puss in Boots

Once upon a time there was a poor miller who had three sons.

When the miller died, the first two sons greedily took everything and left the house. They only left behind the cat for the third son. The son was very sad. He loved his father the most and wept for him and said, "I have nothing but this cat! I will eat him and then soon, I shall die too!" Hearing this, the cat said, "Master, please give me a bag full of carrots and grain and see what great wonders I can do! Please give me a coat and your boots, too!" The miller's son gave the cat all that he asked for.

Puss in Boots

now set off for the jungle. He laid a trap with carrots in it and caught a rabbit. Puss in Boots also caught a couple of partridges with the grain his master had given him. Puss in Boots then went to meet the king. He presented the partridges and rabbit to the king and said, "Your Majesty! These are gifts from my master, the Marquis of Carabas!" The king was very pleased with the gifts.

On his way back home, Puss in Boots passed by some fields where harvesters were working in the sun. He commanded them, "If anyone asks you whom this field belongs to, you must reply that

it belongs to the Marquis of Carabas! If you do not agree, I will get the ogre to eat you all up!" The workers were frightened of the ogre and agreed to do so.

When Puss in Boots reached home, he told his master, "Master, you will be meeting the king soon! Do as I say. Go to the river nearby and have a bath!" The man did as his cat told him to. He took off his clothes and jumped into the river. Puss in Boots immediately took all the clothes and hid behind a rock nearby. When the

king's carriage passed by, the cat went up to the king and said, "Your Majesty! My master is drowning! Some thugs robbed him of his fine clothes and pushed him into this river! Please save him!" The king, on hearing this, commanded his servants, "Save the Marquis of Carabas and give him the finest clothes to wear!" They did as he told them. The cat and his master were very happy. Now, when the carriage went past the fields, the king stopped by and asked the workers, "To whom do these fields belong?" They replied, "The Marquis of Carabas,

Your Majesty!" The king was very pleased to hear this.

Puss in Boots, in the meantime, ran ahead of the king's carriage. He went to the castle nearby. There lived a ferocious ogre. The cat said to him, "I have heard of your mighty powers! I have heard you can become anything you want to!" The ogre laughed and decided to show Puss in Boots all his powers. He replied, "Of course!" and instantly turned into a lion. Then the ogre became a monkey and finally became his real self. Now, the clever cat challenged, "I am sure you cannot become one of

the tiniest creatures in the world! You can never become a mouse!" The ogre was enraged and said, "Watch this!" Saying this, he turned into a tiny mouse. Puss in Boots quickly pounced on him and ate him up!

When the king and the miller's son reached the castle, the cat said, "Welcome, Your Majesty! This is the castle of the Marquis of Carabas!" Hearing this, the king was very pleased. He asked the miller's son to marry his youngest and loveliest daughter. The miller's son knew that the king's daughter was very beautiful and agreed.

Soon, they were married and lived happily ever after in the castle.

## 1 The Seven Ravens

A man had seven strong sons but he longed for a daughter. Eventually, a girl was born to his wife. He sent his sons to fetch water for her baptism. On the way back, one of the boys dropped the jug in the well. Now all of them were too afraid to return home. Angry by the delay, the man cursed that all his sons turn into ravens.

Meanwhile, the little girl grew up to be a beautiful and strong girl. One day, she heard people saying, "You had seven brothers. But your father cursed them to become ravens. Now, you are the only one who can save them." She was determined to find her brothers. She took a ring belonging to her parents and set off.

After some days, she came to the glass mountain where her brothers were locked. Unable to find a key, she cut off one of her fingers to open the lock. When she went inside, she found seven plates of food and seven glasses of water on the table. The little sister ate a morsel of food from each plate and took a sip of water from each glass. But in the last little glass she dropped the ring and then went and hid inside.

Suddenly, she heard the flutter of wings. The ravens had returned. They sat down to eat. "Look at this!" the seventh raven picked up the ring in his glass, and recognised it immediately. "I wish our sister was here. If she touched us we'd be free." The girl came forward and she touched them lovingly. At once they were restored to their human forms again.

## 2 The Eagle and the Woodcutter

Once upon a time there was a kind woodcutter. One day, when he was returning from the forest after a hard day's work, he saw a beautiful eagle caught in a trap.

The woodcutter was so overwhelmed by its majestic beauty that he set the eagle free. The eagle flapped its wings happily, looked at the woodcutter in gratitude, and flew away.

A few months later, the woodcutter was sitting on a rock at the top of a steep hill. When he sat down to have his lunch, suddenly an eagle came down at great speed from the sky and flew away with his hat. The man got up at once and ran down the hill after the bird, hoping to get back his hat. Suddenly, he heard a loud crash behind him. The rock on which he was sitting went rolling down the hill and crashed with a thunderous sound.

Then he looked at the eagle. It was the same eagle and had saved the woodcutter's life.

# 3 Katie and the Mirror

Katie was a silly girl. She would often get a beating from her mother for making stupid mistakes but she never learnt from them.

One day, she went for a walk in the woods. When she grew tired, she sat down near a lake to eat a sandwich. After that she fell asleep.

When she woke up, it was very dark. She could not see her reflection in the water. And silly Katie thought that since she could not see herself, she was lost. Finally, after wandering around for some time, she reached home and knocked on the door and asked, "Is Katie inside?" A voice from inside said, "She must be in her bedroom." Silly Katie thought that if Katie was inside then she must be someone else. So she went away and never returned.

# 4 John the Simpleton

John was a very simple boy. He returned home after a party at his friend's house one day, to see his parents and his younger brother and sister very ill. They had eaten poisonous mushrooms and were in great pain. "Quick! Run to the pharmacy and get some medicine," asked John's father. He told John to tell the pharmacist what the problem was and to get a dose of medicine for four people.

John left but did not return for a long time.

His family waited and waited and his parents began to worry about him. Thankfully, after a while, John's father began to feel a little better and decided to go and look for John. He found John lying on the roadside, holding his stomach and writhing in pain. "What happened?" asked his father. Poor John replied, "I don't know father. I did what you asked me to. I went to the pharmacy and got four doses of medicine and took them all."

## 5 The She-Wolf and the Fox

One day, a she-wolf invited a fox to be the godfather to her newborn and for dinner. They decided to look after the little cub together. After the meal was over, the fox told her that the cub was hungry and that they should get some food for it. He took her near a sheep-fold and asked her to bring a sheep and said that he would bring a chicken. But the wily fox just sat and rested. When the she-wolf went to the sheep-fold, the peasants poured hot water over her. She managed to escape and ran to the fox. He told her that the farmers had beaten him up and made her carry him back to his house. There he jumped off her back and laughed at her and said, "Farewell, I hope your burns have taught you a lesson!"

## 6 The One-Eyed Giant

Once there lived a giant who had a long blade of iron called the giant's knife. He had only one eye in the middle of his forehead. He used to grind the bones of his victims and make bread out of it.

The giant captured a small boy named Jack, one day, but he didn't grind his bones. Instead, he made Jack his servant. For years Jack served the giant. He tried hard to escape but could not. The giant also kept a ferocious dog.

One day, Jack found the giant sleeping after a heavy meal. His knife lay in his hand but in sleep he had loosened his grip on the knife.

Jack saw this as a good opportunity to get rid of the wicked giant and escape. He quietly took the knife and pierced it into the giant's eye. The giant howled in pain and died instantly. Jack also killed his dog that was sleeping nearby.

Then Jack quickly opened the door and ran away and never came back.

## 7 The Three Little Birds

Once there lived three sisters. The eldest sister was married to the king while the two younger ones were married to his ministers.

The eldest sister was about to bear a child. But the king had to be away. The younger sisters had no children. The jealous sisters threw the newborn boy into the river. When the king returned they said, "Our sister gave birth to a dog so we threw him away." The king was sad. The second son also met the same fate. The third time a girl was born and this time they said, "The queen is bewitched. She has given birth to a cat." The king was furious and shut the queen in prison. Three birds who lived on a tree by the river saw the wicked sisters drowning the infants.

Meanwhile, a fisherman brought up all the children who had been thrown in the river. When the eldest son came to know he said, "I will go out and search for our parents." When he did not return, his younger brother left to search for him but did not return either. At last, the sister said, "I must look for my brothers. They must be in trouble." She found her brothers wandering in the forest. They all returned home to the fisherman's joy. One day while hunting, the king met the second son in the forest. The boy took the king to his house. Seeing the king, the magical birds sang the whole story— that the fisherman's children were actually the king's children who had been thrown into the river. The king was stunned by the song and realised his mistake. He at once released the queen. "Please forgive me, my queen," he begged her. and ordered for the wicked sisters to be thrown in a well.

## 8 Redfeathers, the Hen

Redfeathers was a hen. All her feathers were red. One day, a fox saw Redfeathers and decided to eat it for dinner. "Keep the water boiling. I'm going to bring a plump chicken for dinner," he told his wife. So, the fox went to catch Redfeathers and before she could realise what he was doing, he grabbed and pushed her into a sack. The hen's friend, the dove had seen what had happened to his friend. "Oh, I must save my friend," he thought. The dove came flapping down on the fox's path, "Oh, my wings! My lovely wings!" He pretended as if his wings were broken. The greedy fox put the sack down and chased the dove that went further and further away.

Meanwhile, Redfeathers slipped out of the sack, put a stone inside it, and escaped. The fox carried the sack home and turned it over the boiling pot. "Splash!" Hot water fell on the greedy fox. Howling in pain he slunk away to a corner.

## 9 The Two Daughters

Once a man had two daughters. The first one was married to a farmer and the second one married a potter.

One day, the father visited the first daughter and asked her if everything was well with her. The daughter nodded and replied, "We grow a lot of grains and vegetables in our field. Every night I pray to God that it rains so that our crops can have enough water. She said,"Father, please pray for rains."

Then the father went to the second daughter and asked her if everything was fine. The second daughter happily answered, "We make pots with clay and then keep them for drying in the sun. Every night I pray to God that it does not rain because if it rains our pots would be spoilt. Father, please pray that it does not rain."

The old man didn't know what to pray for.

## 10 The Sparrows and the Elephant

Two sparrows lived in a nest on a tree. One morning, a wild elephant broke the branch on which their nest was built. All their eggs were destroyed but the sparrows flew away to safety.

The sparrows friend, the woodpecker, consoled them and said that she would think of a way to kill the elephant. She asked the gnat for help who in turn told them to take the frog's help. The clever frog told the gnat to buzz near the elephant's ears who would then close its eyes to listen to the music. Then the woodpecker would pluck its eyes out, and the frog would lead the elephant to the pit by its croaking.

The plan was put into action the next day. The elephant, after being blinded by the woodpecker, fell down into the pit and died and the sparrows were very happy.

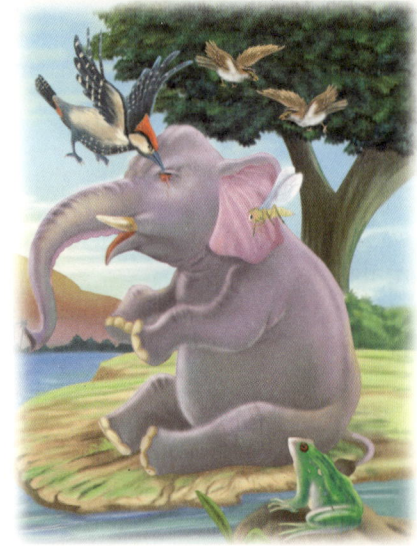

## 11 The Goat and the Fox

Once a fox fell into a well. He saw a goat passing by and called out to her. He tricked her by saying that he was in the well because the water tasted good. The goat believed the fox and she too jumped into the well. The clever fox promised to help her come out. He climbed on the goat and got out of the well and ran away. The poor goat was left in the water and realised her mistake.

# 12 The Strange Flower

A king had a beautiful daughter but she could not speak. She silently took care of plants and flowers in the royal garden.

One day, the princess found a strange flower in her garden. Every day, she tended to the flower. She could even talk to the flower!

The king saw his daughter talking to the flower and become upset. He thought that a witch had planted the flower in the royal garden. He told the servants to throw the flower away. While they were digging the plant out, it fell to the ground. The flower turned into a handsome prince! He said, "Sire, I really love your daughter. I changed into a flower so that I could be with her every day!"

The king was very happy and the prince and princess were married and lived happily ever after.

# 13 Doctor Know-All

Humphrey wanted to become a doctor. So, one day, he wore a black coat and put a signboard saying "Doctor Know-all" outside his home.

One day, a rich man was robbed of his money. He went to Doctor Know-all and said, "Since your name is Doctor Know-all, you know who robbed me! Please come to my home for dinner tonight." At dinnertime, the servants started serving the food. Seeing the first servant, the doctor said, "Oh, good! Here comes the first!" This scared the servant, who was actually one of the robbers.

The same thing happened with the second servant, who was the other robber. Thinking that they have been caught, the servants fell on their knees and apologized and returned all the stolen money. Everyone praised Doctor Know-all's intelligence!

## 14 Diamonds and Toads

A widow had two daughters. She liked her eldest daughter who was proud and sour but hated the younger daughter who was sweet-natured. One day, when the younger sister had gone to fetch water, a poor old woman asked for water. The gentle girl gave her water. The woman blessed her saying, "Whenever you speak, jewels and flowers will come out of your mouth." This woman was actually a fairy.

She told her mother all that had happened. This time, the widow sent her elder daughter to fetch water. When a well-dressed lady asked her for water, the girl spoke rudely to her. The fairy cursed her that toads and snakes would come out of her mouth whenever she spoke. When she returned home, her mother was horrified to see her condition. She was thrown out of the house.

Meanwhile, the younger daughter met a prince who was awestruck by her beauty and married her.

## 15 The Ass's Test

Once a man went to the market nearby to buy an ass. There, he saw an animal that looked somewhat like an ass and bought him on trial. He came back and put the new animal in the stable along with the other asses.

One day, the man noticed that the animal sat beside the laziest and greediest ass in the stable. Seeing this, the man at once put a halter on the animal and took him back to its original owner.

The seller was quite taken aback to see the animal back and wondered how could the man test him so soon. The man replied, "I have tested him and have come to know what kind of an animal it is. It will be of no use to me as it is very lazy and greedy." The seller asked him how he could be so sure. The man replied, "Everyone can be judged from the company he chooses."

# 16 The Gingerbread Man

A little old man and a little old woman stayed in a cottage.

One day, the woman made a gingerbread man for dinner. She decorated the gingerbread man with eyes made of currants and buttons made of cherries. But when she took out gingerbread man from the oven, he jumped out and ran away.

The old woman and her husband ran after him but gingerbread man was too fast for them. Neither the pig, nor the cow, nor the horse who followed, could outrun gingerbread man. Now, the gingerbread man came to a river and didn't know how to cross it. A sly fox came up to him and offered to help him to cross the river. He asked him to sit on his tail but gingerbread man began to get wet. Then the fox told him to sit on his back and finally on his nose.

No sooner did gingerbread man sit on the fox's nose, that the sly fox tossed him and gobbled him up.

# 17 The Goose Girl

A beautiful princess was on her way to marry a prince who lived far away. "Keep this handkerchief with you. It will protect you against all evil," said her mother bidding her goodbye. The princess was accompanied by her maid-in-waiting. Unknown to all, the maid was a wicked witch. They both rode on horses but the princess's horse was special. He was a speaking horse called Falada.

A while later the princess requested, "I am thirsty. Can you bring me water?" The maid refused. And alas! When the princess bent to drink water the handkerchief fell in it and was swept away. "Aha! Now your powers have gone!" exulted the maid. She made the princess wear shabby clothes and give up Falada. She then disguised herself as the princess and entered the prince's kingdom.

She married the prince and sent the real princess to work with the goose boy. "Behead Falada!" ordered the new bride so that nobody would come to know the truth. But at the real princess's request, the head of the horse was nailed at the gateway so that she could see it whenever she took the geese out. Every day the horse would relate the princess's story. The goose boy heard the horse and informed the king. "One day, the king. heard the horse and came to know about the reality. The false bride was sentenced to death while the real princess was married to the prince and they lived happily ever after.

## 18 The Golden Clog

Once a shoe seller was selling clogs in a village. He went up and down the road shouting at the top of his voice. The villagers were very annoyed. "Let us buy everything he has on sale and send him back," they decided. But, the people noticed that no matter how much they bought, his basket was never empty. "The shoe seller must be a magician!" said one man.

The matter was taken to the king. The shoe seller made a golden clog and gifted it to the prince. The king was very pleased and rewarded the shoe seller. Thereafter, the shoe seller disappeared.

Alas! Nobody could get the clog off from the prince's foot. The clog grew in size along with the prince's foot but it never caused him any discomfort. Years passed by.

The prince was married. Now the clog began to hurt and only stopped causing pain when the marriage was broken.

One day, a magician visited the king's court. "The prince will be happy if he marries the girl who can take the golden clog off from his feet," he declared. Many princesses from far and wide came to try their luck but in vain. Finally a scullery maid came to try her luck. Everyone laughed at her and made fun. But lo! The maiden kissed the clog and it came off!

The maiden was actually the shoe seller's daughter and changed into a lovely princess as soon as the clog came off the prince's feet.

The king was very happy and the prince was married to the lovely princess.

## 19 The Old Man and His Grandson

Once there was a man. He was so old that he could not even hold his spoon properly and would spill food on the table. His son and daughter-in-law, with whom he lived, did not like this, so they started giving him food in an earthen bowl.

The old man would always sit in a corner of the room and look at the food on the table with yearning eyes. One day, the earthen bowl dropped from his trembling hands and broke into pieces. The son and his wife were very angry and gave him a wooden bowl to eat from.

One day, the old man's grandson was collecting some wood. When his father asked him why he was doing so, he replied, "I will make bowls with this wood and give you food in them when you grow old."

The old man's son and daughter-in-law immediately realised their mistake and brought the old man to the table and asked him to forgive them. From that day, the family ate together.

## 20 The Camel and the Jackal

A camel and a jackal were very good friends. One day, the jackal asked the camel to carry him across the river to a sugarcane field.

Once they reached the sugarcane field, the jackal hurriedly ate up all the sugarcane before the camel could lay his hands on even one. Then he created a great noise and ran away from the field. The villagers rushed to the field to see what had happened. Seeing the camel, the villagers thought he had eaten up all their sugarcane. They gathered sticks and beat him black and blue.

The camel realised how wicked his friend has been and decided to teach him a lesson. While swimming back, he shook his shoulders so hard that the jackal fell from his shoulders and was drowned in the water.

## 21 The Hare's Bride

A woman and her daughter grew many cabbages in their garden. A hare used to eat up all the cabbages.

One day, the girl went up to the hare and told him to keep away from the cabbages. He replied, "First, sit on my little tail and come to my little hut." She refused to listen to him. The same thing happened the next day.

The third time, the girl agreed to do as the hare demanded. When they reached the hut, he asked her to cook green cabbage and millet seed for their wedding as he intended to marry her.

The girl was very sad and did not wish to marry the hare. She locked herself inside the kitchen and sat in a corner and wept.

Suddenly, she had an idea. She dressed a straw doll in her clothes, put a spoon in its hand and placed it by the pan. When she found the hare busy in his work, she silently escaped and found her way back home.

## 22 The Fox with the Stunted Tail

One day, while roving in the forests, a fox's tail got trapped in a trap. He pulled himself so hard that the tail snapped and remained in the trap.

He became very depressed for losing the most precious part of his body. When he saw the other foxes, he felt it was unjust that all of them should roam about flaunting their bushy tails when he couldn't do so.

So he made a plan and went up to them and said, "The tail is a useless extension of our body because it does not serve any purpose. Besides, it also looks bad and ugly. So, you should all cut off your tails like I have done."

His peers understood how jealous he had grown and said, "Then why are you looking so unhappy without one?"

## 23 The Wedding of Mrs. Fox

Once upon a time there lived a wicked old fox. Every day he used to catch rats and eat them all by himself, not leaving even a morsel for his wife, Mrs. Fox. Soon, Mrs. Fox grew weak and thin. Her only friend in the house was Little Cat, who urged her to leave Mr. Fox and marry somebody else.

One day, Mr. Fox overheard Little Cat and Mrs. Fox's having a discussion. He hatched a plan to teach his wife a lesson.

One day, he pretended to be dead and lay down on his bed. Everyone thought that he had died. After that, many suitors came to woo Mrs. Fox, but she refused to marry any of them.

Finally, a wolf arrived and asked for Mrs. Fox's hand. He also promised to share all his food with her. Tempted by this offer, Mrs. Fox agreed to the marriage. On the day of the wedding, Mr. Fox attacked the wolf, but the wolf being stronger, killed him.

Finally, Mrs. Fox married the wolf.

## 24 Ali Baba and the Forty Thieves

Ali Baba was a poor woodcutter. He barely managed to feed his family a single meal with the money that he earned every day.

One day, while cutting wood in a forest, he heard the deafening sound of hooves approaching him. He turned around. A huge dust storm, raised by a troop of horsemen, was coming his way. Ali Baba quickly hid himself behind a boulder and watched the men.

He found a group of forty thieves with their booty, alighting from their horses. Then one of them went up to a cave and cried out loud, "Open Sesame." What he saw next left Ali Baba dumbfounded. The gates of the rock opened and the forty thieves walked inside with their loot. After some time, they came out and one of the robbers cried, "Close Sesame," and the gates closed.

Ali Baba waited until the thieves rode away. Then emerging from behind the boulder, he walked up to the cave nervously and said, "Open Sesame."

The cave opened and Ali Baba walked inside. Instead of a dark and dingy cave, there lay before him a treasure trove. He found bags filled with gold coins, diamonds, and other precious gems. Overjoyed, Ali Baba quickly gathered whatever he could and fled from the forest.

He reached home and showed his wife all the treasures. They became rich overnight and from then onwards he and his family lived happily. Ali Baba never returned to the cave. However, now that he was a rich man, he generously helped his needy friends with the money.

## 25 The Snow Maiden

Once there was an old man who lived with his wife. They were very sad because they had no children.

One winter, when it was snowing, they made a beautiful statue of a girl with snow. Then they wished it would become a real girl. And lo! Their wish came true; the statue became a beautiful little girl. They were very happy as she played around the house all day. The winter passed by in happiness but as spring came the girl became sad and quiet. When summer came, she became sadder and quieter than before.

One day, the old man and woman asked their little girl to go to the forest with her friends as they thought that it would lift her spirits and make her happy once again. The group of girls went to the forest and picked flowers. Then they made a fire and danced around it. But as soon as the little girl went near the fire, she melted down and evaporated into thin air.

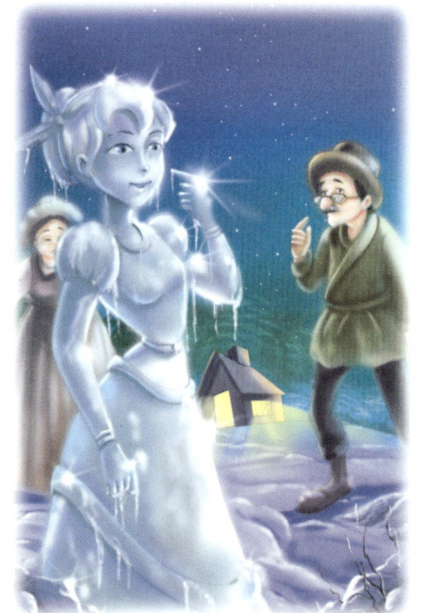

## 26 Apollo and the Shepherd

Apollo is the Greek god of music. Whenever he played his lyre, people stood spellbound. One day, Apollo came to know of Olander, a shepherd, who was an expert flautist. Apollo grew jealous and decided to challenge Olander to a contest.

They played before a packed crowd who were mesmerised by their melodious tunes. Finally, when even the judges could not decide whom to crown as the winner, Apollo said he would play the lyre upside down. Once again beautiful tunes flowed from the instrument as Apollo played. Now it was Olander's turn to play his instrument from the other end, but when he blew no sound came from it.

While everybody cheered Apollo, Olander understood that he was tricked because unlike a lyre a flute can never be played from the opposite end of the mouthpiece.

## 27 The Caged Dove

One day, a girl lost her way in the woods. Searching for a way out she came to a caged dove. The dove was actually a prince who was turned into a dove by a wicked witch. "I will help you out of the woods. But you must first fulfil my wish," said the dove. "The key to this cage is in the witch's house. You have to recover it and unlock the cage." The girl agreed and crept into the witch's house. Just as she was about to come out with the key, the witch saw her. The terrified girl rushed back and hurriedly opened the cage. Suddenly, there appeared a young prince in place of the dove. When the witch arrived to catch the girl, the prince cut off her head with his sword.

Joyfully, the prince and the girl went back home. The king was glad to find his son safe. The prince and the girl get married and they lived happily ever after.

## 28 The Ungrateful Son

A man and his wife were sitting to eat roast chicken for dinner. Suddenly, the man saw his old father approaching. He hid the chicken because he did not want to share it. The father had a drink and went away.

When the son took out the chicken, it had turned into a toad. The toad jumped and stuck forever to the man's face. He was punished for being ungrateful.

## 29 The Giant and the Miser

Once there lived a kindhearted giant. One day, he came to know of a blacksmith who treated his workers unjustly. He decided to teach him a lesson.

The giant went to ask the blacksmith for work. "How much money do I need to pay you?" asked the blacksmith. "Give me whatever you can for each blow of the hammer," said the giant. The blacksmith was overjoyed for he would pay only a meager amount and get all the work done by the giant.

Once the deal was settled, the giant took the hammer and gave such a blow that the anvil broke into pieces. The blacksmith grew worried and decided to do away with the giant. He asked the giant how much he should pay him for that single blow. "Just this," said the giant and kicked the blacksmith hard sending him flying over the rooftop.

## 30 How the Rabbit Became White

One day, a Red Indian tribesman, named Eye of the Eagle, decided to go hunting to get food for his tribe. On reaching the forest, he discovered that all the animals had fled to the snow-capped peaks since it was very hot and they were unable to bear the summer heat in the plains.

Worried about how to feed his tribe hence, Eye of the Eagle immediately set out for the mountains to catch some animals.

On his way up the mountains, a blizzard arose and he lost his way. As the snow fell more heavily, he was completely stranded. Suddenly he met a brown rabbit that helped him reach his house.

Eye of the Eagle was so grateful that he chanted a magic spell and turned the rabbit from brown to white to save it from being hunted down in the snow.

# Contents

*The Story of the Month:   The Snow Queen*

The Story of the Month

# The Snow Queen

## The Snow Queen

Once upon a time there lived a wicked goblin who built a magic mirror. Anything that was beautiful or good was reflected in it as ugly and bad. One day, the mirror broke and all its pieces fell all over the earth. A few pieces also fell in a small town where two friends named Kay and Gerda lived.

Kay and Gerda were neighbours. They were very good friends and spent their days playing games, building sand blocks and running across the sun-kissed fields.

One day while they were playing, bits of the broken mirror hit Kay's eyes and one piece pierced his heart. After that everything changed. Kay no longer viewed Gerda as his best friend. He poked fun at her and hit her on the head whenever he could. Gerda was puzzled and couldn't understand why he was behaving in such a strange way.

One day, Kay and his group of friends decided to go on a sledge ride over the snow. Suddenly, a huge sledge drew up before him and its driver asked him to step in. Once Kay was inside, the driver transformed himself into a woman and sped away. She was draped in a white flowing gown and on her head was placed a crown made of ice. Her silky white locks cascaded like a flowing stream. Astonished Kay asked her who she was. "I am the Snow Queen," replied the woman, whose face shone like a sparkling diamond. She tugged at the reins and rode past the clouds and the rainbow, till they reached a distant land.

Meanwhile, Gerda waited for Kay to return. One day, she took her boat and went to search for him in the river. Seeing Gerda, a fairy cast her magic spell and made the boat approach her. When Gerda narrated her

story, she sent her garden flowers everywhere to search for Kay, but they returned empty-handed.

Gerda sat under a tree and wept all night. Suddenly a crow flew down and informed her about a certain princess who had recently married a boy. Gerda grew restless thinking that Kay had married someone else and urged the crow to take her to the princess's palace. Gerda waited anxiously inside the palace and when the boy entered she sighed with relief because it wasn't Kay.

Gerda carried on her search and came to

a forest where she met a robber girl and her reindeer. Hearing Gerda's sad tale, the reindeer said he had seen the Snow Queen flying away with a boy to Lapland. She immediately set out for Lapland and the reindeer accompanied her. There, they came across a magician who told them that Kay was at the Snow Queen's palace and owing to the piece of glass inside him, he considered it to be the best place in the world. She suggested Gerda visit the palace.

The Snow Queen's palace was made out of ice. It was cold and dark, and no one except

the Snow Queen lived in it. One day, she challenged Kay to spell the word "Eternity" from an assorted chunk of alphabets, all made of ice, and promised him his freedom in return.

Kay wracked his brains hard but just couldn't spell the word. Just then Gerda arrived and seeing her long-lost friend she cried out in joy and embraced him. Just as her warm tears fell on his hard cheeks Kay felt his cold heart begin melting. He recognized Gerda and wept aloud. Suddenly, a teardrop fell on the alphabets and they spelt out the word "Eternity."

Kay was set free and he went back home with Gerda.

# 1 Three Little Men in the Wood

Dorothy went to collect strawberries in the forest. On her way, she met three little men in the forest. "We are hungry. Will you share your food?" they asked. Dorothy gave them the bread she was carrying. Impressed by her kindness, the three men gave her a boon each. One said, "You will get prettier every day." The second said, "You will be very rich." "You will marry a king," said the third. Dorothy was very happy. She returned home and told her stepmother what had happened in the forest.

The jealous stepmother sent her ugly daughter with a loaf of bread to the forest. She too met the three men who asked her for food, but she rudely refused to share it with them. Angry, they all cursed her saying that she would get uglier, have two horns on her head and die a miserable death.

Many years passed by and one day, Dorothy met a king passing by. He fell in love with her and married her. He took her away to his kingdom.

The stepmother could not bear this. One night, she killed Dorothy and placed her own daughter on the king's bed. Before leaving she covered her face so that the king might not see her face. However, the king lifted the cloth and saw the horns.

Meanwhile, the queen had turned into a swan. She was swimming in the palace pond when the king saw her. "Sire, brandish your sword over me," she bade him. Lo! The king was astonished to see his queen before him. He banished the stepmother and her daughter from his kingdom.

# 2 Why Dogs Wag Their Tails

Once a merchant had a cat and a dog. The dog had served his master well. But now that it was old, his only task was to guide the young cat. One day, the merchant decided to send his daughter a magic ring. He ordered the cat to carry the ring in his mouth and the dog to guide the cat to his daughter's house. The cat and the dog obediently left.

On the way, they came across a river that had to be crossed. Thinking that the cat might lose the ring, the dog snatched it from him. However, while crossing the river, the dog himself dropped it midway.

When the cat told the master about the ring, the angry master sent other dogs to bite off the culprit's tail.

Since then, whenever a dog meets another of its species it asks, "Are you the one who lost the ring?" The dog replies with a wag of its tail to prove that he is not the guilty one.

This is why dogs always wag their tails.

## 3 The Wolf and the Heron

One day while eating a fish, a bone got stuck in a wolf's throat. He howled in pain and saw a heron roaming nearby and called out for help. When the heron came closer, the wolf explained his problem and said that he would reward the heron if he saved his life.

The heron put his long beak into the wolf's throat and took out the fish bone. The wolf thanked the heron for saving his life and was about to leave when the heron asked, "Where is the reward that you had promised to give me in return for saving your life?"

The wolf turned and smiled and replied, "I have not eaten you, isn't that a reward in itself."

Saying this the wolf went away and the heron realised that wolves are very selfish and do not keep their word.

## 4 The Hawk and the Hen

One day, a hawk saw a pretty hen and fell in love with her and wanted to marry her. The hen agreed at once and they decided to get engaged. While leaving, the hawk gave her a ring and flew away. Now the hen had also agreed to marry a cock. When the cock saw her wearing the ring, he was angry and told her he would kill her if she married the hawk. Frightened, the hen immediately removed the ring and threw it away.

After a few days when the hawk returned to marry the hen, he noticed that the ring was no longer on her finger. The hen came up with the excuse that a snake had snatched it from her and she was still looking for it.

The hawk watched her closely and knew that she was lying. He said, "As a punishment for your deception you shall keep scratching this earth till you find the ring."

Since that day, hens have the habit of scratching the ground.

## 5 The Alligator's Fruit

Two women went to an orchard to pick fruits. This orchard belonged to an alligator. While eating the fruits, one of them said, "Don't throw any peel with your teeth marks on it as the alligator will see it and will come to know that we were here." However, the other woman did not listen and did exactly that. The alligator saw the peel and recognised the woman.

The next day, he went to the village and asked the villagers to give her up to him. The villagers asked him to wait a while. They went inside and heated an iron rod over the flames. Coming out they asked the alligator to open his mouth and when he did, they pushed the burning rod in saying, "Here's your fruit!"

## 6 The Tree with Agate Beads

One day, a man and his dog went to hunt in the woods. There the man shot an arrow at a beautiful deer but the animal quickly escaped into a cave.

The man followed the animal into the dark cave. The animal went deeper and deeper into the cave and the man followed. Soon he realised that he was hopelessly lost and couldn't find his way out. A while later, he heard his dog barking. Following the sound, he felt his way in the darkness. His hands touched a tree, which seemed to have berries on it. When the man broke off a branch, the tree began to talk! The frightened man ran out as fast as he could. Outside, he discovered that the berries on the branch were actually precious agate beads.

When the people heard the story they went in search of the tree. Instead they found that evil sprits had taken it away and had left strange carvings on the walls of the cave that are there even today.

# 7 Faithful John

An old king was gravely ill and going to die. He told John, his faithful servant, "Look after my son after my death but do not show him the picture of the princess in the gallery otherwise he will fall in love with her and commit many crimes to get her." John promised to obey. A few days later, the king died.

One day, the young king saw the picture of the princess and fell in love with her. He took John and set off in a ship with gifts for the princess. The princess was impressed with the king and pleased with the gifts. The king confessed his great love for her and she agreed to marry him.

During their journey back, John overheard the conversation of three ravens. They were talking about the dangers the king would face. But whoever told him about these dangers would be turned into stone. The queen fainted during the bridal dance and John brought her back to life by sucking three drops of blood from her heart as the ravens had told him to do. But the king was furious with him and he ordered that John be hanged for touching the queen. Before dying, John told him about the conversation of the ravens. Hearing this, the king asked for forgiveness but it was too late—John turned into stone.

The king and the queen were sorry for what happened. One day, John's stone figure said to the king, "You can bring me back to life if you cut your son's heads off and sprinkle their blood on me." The king repaid John's loyalty by doing as he asked. John came back to life and rewarded the king by restoring his son's lives and they all lived happily ever after.

# 8 Hanaca's Hat

Once there lived a famous samurai warrior and his beautiful daughter Hanaca. He covered her head with a strange hat that hid her face. People ridiculed her funny hat and laughed at her. Unable to bear their remarks, she fled her country and became a king's maid in a neighbouring country.

Hanaca soon pleased everybody with her work and the prince too fell in love with her. However, the king opposed this friendship as she was a mere servant and banished Hanaca from his kingdom. She was about to leave when a great wind blew away her hat and revealed her exquisite face. Everyone in the palace stood stupefied to see her face and her head, which was covered with precious jewels.

One of the king's courtiers recognised her as the daughter of the samurai and told the king. The king then arranged for Hanaca's marriage to the prince.

## 9  A Hut in the Forest

A poor woodcutter had four daughters. One day, he went to the forest to get some wood and asked his eldest daughter to bring him his lunch. He told her that he would strew breadcrumbs on the way so that she might follow them and find him.

However, when she set out for the forest, there were no breadcrumbs anywhere! The birds had eaten them and the girl got lost in the forest. While she was wandering about, she came upon a hut in which an old man and his pets used to live. He took pity on her and gave her shelter and asked her to cook a meal for him. But the girl was very rude and ate up all the food that she had cooked. At night the old man asked her to make the bed for the others, but she only made her own bed and went off to sleep. The old man was furious and locked her in a dark room.

Soon, two of the woodcutter's other daughters went to the forest to look for their sister. They also came upon the same hut and met the old man. When he asked them to cook food and make the beds, they disobeyed his orders. In anger, he locked them up as well.

Finally, the youngest daughter began to worry and went to the forest to look for her elder sisters. When she came to the old man's hut and was told to cook food and make the beds, she obediently did as she was told.

The next morning, she woke up to find a handsome prince instead of the old man and married him and they lived happily ever after.

## 10  Alan and the Hunters

Two hunters killed a wild pig, but they had no fire on which to cook it. So they went to look for some fire and saw a house nearby. They found a man called Alan and his baby sleeping inside the house. They asked Alan to help them light a fire. Alan helped them and in return, asked them to give him a little meat for his baby after they had cooked it. Saying so, Alan left for work.

The men agreed to do so. But they were very hungry and ate up all the meat themselves. Then the wicked men hid the baby.

When Alan returned home, he found his baby missing. He searched the whole house but didn't find his baby anywhere. Then he ran to the spot where the two men were. Finding them hiding in a tree, he picked up an axe and chopped the tree. The hunters fell to the ground and died instantly.

Later, Alan discovered a lot of treasure buried where the baby was hidden and became rich.

## 11 The Sun and the Moon

One day, the Sun and the Moon had a quarrel as to who was the stronger of the two.

The two argued with each other for ages and finally the Sun declared that the Moon could not shine if the Sun's light did not fall on it and illuminate it. To prove his might and utility, the Moon proudly replied, "You burn the earth with your heat and give light, but when I shine at night women come outdoors to spin in the moonlight."

On hearing this, the Sun became so angry that he picked up some mud and flung it at the Moon's face. The Moon tried to get out of the way but couldn't and the mud got stuck to him.

It is believed that since then the Moon has dark spots on its face, where the Sun threw mud at it.

## 12 The Turtle and the Lizard

Once a turtle and a lizard went to steal some ginger from a house. The owner of the house chased the animals with a stick. The lizard scurried away to a secure place leaving the turtle behind. Finally, the turtle managed to find a coconut shell and saved himself from the owner. Unable to find the animals, the man left.

Next, the turtle showed the lizard a honeycomb. Once again the greedy lizard ran ahead of his friend to grab the first bite but he did not see the bees near the honeycomb. After being attacked by the bees, the lizard howled in pain and came to his friend for help. Now the turtle understood how greedy the lizard was. So he showed him a trap and said that it was a silver necklace that his grandfather had gifted him. This time too, the lizard ran ahead to grab it, but got trapped instead. It begged the turtle to set him free but the turtle wanted to punish the lizard and refused to do so. The lizard learnt his lesson.

## 13 Pea Blossom

Five peas lived inside a green shell. The first four were arrogant while the last one was humble and kind hearted. They were happily spending their days when one day, the farmer came and plucked them. "What will happen to us?" the peas grew unsure of their fate.

One day, they found themselves in the hands of a child who began throwing them in all directions. While one fell into the gutter; the other went flying towards the sun; the other two fell before a pigeon that ate them instantly. The last pea however fell inside a hut where a poor woman lived with her sick child. The mother had given up all hopes for her daughter's survival.

"Mother, look! There is a pea on the floor," beamed the child. There was a glow in the girl's pale cheeks. "Will you plant it outside my window?" As the pea took roots and grew, sprouting new leaves, the child too recovered.

## 14 Mistaken Gifts

A boy called Saigon lived in a village with his parents. His parents wanted him to get married and finally decided upon a beautiful maiden who lived in the neighbouring village. A man was sent to the girl's house to tell her parents that Saigon would like to marry their daughter. When the man reached their house he found them nodding their heads while relishing a meal. The man thought this was a sign that they had agreed to the wedding and rushed home with the news. Overjoyed, Saigon's parents started planning for the wedding. There was a custom in the village that the groom's family had to give many gifts to the girl's family. Saigon's family bought lovely gifts and set off for the neighbouring village. But when they reached there, the girl's family said they were not ready to get their daughter married.

## 15 The Magic Jar

One day, a group of Tinguian huntsmen went out hunting with their dogs. In the forest, they unleashed their dogs and each hunter went his own way. After sometime, they heard a fierce howl and ran to see what had happened. They found one of the dogs holding a huge jar, but when the hunters tried to take it from the dog, the jar disappeared. They ran after the jar but they were not able to catch it.

A while later, tired and exhausted, the hunters sat under a tree. Soon, they heard a voice say, "To get the jar, you have to get the blood of a pig that has no youngone." They found the blood of a pig and the jar appeared again. But just as they tried to grab it the jar escaped into the dark cave. The men ran behind it and entered the cave but could not manage to find the jar in the darkness.

To this day, the Tinguian tribes believe that a magic jar, named Magsawi, can be found in that cave.

## 16 Ripple Gets a Necklace

Ripple the water pixie lived in a pond. She was very pretty and very proud of herself. As Ripple was always showing off, all her friends were fed up with her. "She cuts the water lily leaves to make her dresses and tips my babies off them!" complained the moorhen. "She tied a water beetle and a dragonfly together because the dragonfly wouldn't give her his wings to make a dress," said the water vole

One day, Bufo, a toad, invited everyone to a party. Ripple started planning what she would wear. She wanted to look the prettiest at the party. She cut up five lily leaves. The lilies were upset as the leaves were new. She took some ribbon for her hair from a waterweed. "Next," she said to herself, "I will make myself a necklace out of some snail shells." "No, you won't," cried the snails and they hid themselves. Ripple looked around for something to make her necklace. She spied long jelly-like strands set with little black beads on the water plants. "Perfect," she said and placed the toad spawn around her neck in six rows.

The next day at the party, all the others laughed at her. Ripple wondered why and then she felt something tickling her. The toad spawn necklace had hatched and all the tadpoles were wriggling down her neck! There were dozens of them. Bufo was furious because the toad spawn necklace was made out of her eggs. Ripple ran away in shame and was never vain again.

## 17 Mother Holle

Once there lived a widow. She had a stepdaughter who was very pretty and hardworking, but her own daughter was ugly and lazy. The stepmother was very cruel and wicked.

One day while spinning, her stepdaughter's fingers started to bleed. She dipped the shuttle into the well to wash it but it fell inside. She jumped inside the well to get the shuttle and lost her senses. When she regained her senses, she found herself in a beautiful meadow. Wandering there, she helped a loaf of bread out of the oven when it cried out to her for help. When the apple tree asked her, she shook the apple tree to drop the ripe apples. At last, she reached a house where an old woman called Mother Holle gave her shelter. The girl did all the work but after some time, she longed to go back home. As a reward for her hard work, Mother Holle heaped upon her a shower of golden rain, which clung to her.

When the stepdaughter reached home and narrated her story, her stepmother desired that her own daughter also be blessed with so much wealth. The lazy girl also jumped in the well and soon found herself in a beautiful meadow. But, she neither helped the burning loaf nor did she listen to the apple tree's request. And when she came to Mother Holle's house, she worked hard for one day but soon became lazy and refused to move. She was only thinking of the wealth she would get. So when it was time for her to return home, Mother Holle emptied a kettle full of tar on her that never came off!

## 18 The Wicked Prince

There was once a wicked prince who made the people of his own kingdom suffer and took all their wealth for himself. No one liked the prince.

One day, he decided to put up his own statue in the church. When the priests refused to fulfil his wish, the prince decided to challenge God himself. He flew towards the heavens in his flying ship, which was fitted with guns and a hundred eagles.

When God saw the evil prince, he sent an angel to stop him. However, the wicked prince shot an arrow and killed the angel. But a drop of blood fell from the angel's body onto the ship, causing it to crash.

However, the prince was unhurt and once again gathered his armies to fight God.

This time God sent one little gnat, which buzzed around the prince and finally stung him. Unable to bear the pain the prince went mad. The people were happy to be free of the wicked prince.

# 19 The Man and the Alans

The Tinguian tribe in the Philippines is very superstitious about ghosts, whom they refer to as alans.

One day, a man while journeying through the dense forest heard strange sounds. Looking around he saw a group of ugly alans hanging from a nearby tree, like bats. They had knotted fingers that were placed backwards and twisted feet and wings. The man was very scared seeing the weird creatures and ran to save himself. The alans too followed and soon caught up with him. They told the man that if he could not find them the magic bead named nabaga they would burn down his house.

The man ran home. The Tinguians believe that alans always keep their promises and to this day he is believed to be searching for the magic bead.

# 20 The Stubborn Pig

One day, unable to take her stubborn pig back home, an old woman asked a dog to bite the pig. The dog refused to obey her so she asked a stick to beat the dog. When the stick refused to do so she asked the fire to burn the stick, but the fire also refused. Tired, she asked the water to douse the fire, but the water also refused to listen to her. She then approached an ox, a butcher, a rope, and a rat, but none agreed to help the old woman.

Finally, the old woman asked a cat to help her. The cat asked her to fetch some milk in return. The cat lapped up all the milk, and then began to eat the rat. The rat began chewing the rope, the rope started hanging the butcher and the butcher began killing the ox.

The ox started drinking the water and the water fell on the fire. The fire burnt the stick and the stick beat the dog and when the dog tried to bite the pig, it fled to the old woman's house.

## 21 The Magpie's Nest

Once a clever magpie was building a nest for herself. All the other birds gathered around her to watch her build it and learn how to make one. However, none of them had the patience to watch till the end, and they rushed away to build their own.

The magpie had nearly finished making her nest and needed to add only one more twig, when a turtle dove asked her to add two instead of one. The dove kept bothering her till the magpie got angry and flew away to another tree. The other birds returned to learn the rest of the craft, but unable to find the magpie each bird had to make their own nest.

Their knowledge remained incomplete and this is why different birds have different nests.

## 22 Battle of the Crabs

A number of crabs used to live along the shore. "The waves make so much noise that we are unable to sleep," said one crab. "We should fight and defeat them!" declared another. They gathered their army and were on their way when they met a small shrimp. "Oh, you poor things! You think you can fight with the huge waves? You are too tiny," the shrimp mocked.

The crabs begged the shrimp to fight on their side. While leading the army the shrimp pointed to the spear on his head and said, "This powerful weapon shields me from the waves." The foolish crabs believed him and kept admiring the shrimp for his courage. Then a huge wave came rushing towards them and killed all the crabs, but the clever shrimp survived. He told the sad tale to the crab's children.

Till today, one can find crabs scurrying towards the waves to fight it, but when their courage fails they hurry back to the shore.

# 23 The Elf of the Rose

Once upon a time an invisible elf used to live inside a bright red rose. One day, when the elf was out it began to snow and the rose closed its petals. Unable to get inside, the elf went and sat on a tree.

A beautiful princess and a man were sitting under the tree. The elf heard the man saying that the girl's wicked brother would kill him if he found out about their love for each other. The man was about to leave when the princess plucked the rose and gave it to him. Finding the petals of the rose open, the elf quickly went inside. On the way, the lover met the wicked brother who severed his head and buried it in a pit. The elf was horrified to see such a dastardly act and planned to meet the princess and tell her everything. He hid himself inside the brother's hat and went to the palace with him. At night when the elf buzzed into the princess's ears, she woke up with a start thinking that she was having a bad dream. The elf introduced himself and told her what had happened to her lover and took her to the same spot.

The princess took the head and plucked a small jasmine twig that was growing nearby. Every night, as the princess wept in her room, a jasmine flower would appear on the branch.

One day, the wicked brother grew suspicious of his sister and took the branch to his room. As bees swarmed around the beautiful flower every day, the invisible elf told them about the wicked brother.

One night, all the bees gathered around the brother and stung him to death.

# 24 The Loveliest Rose in the World

A beautiful queen grew only roses in her garden. Yellow, white, pink and red, they dotted her garden and spread their sweet fragrance all around.

One day, the queen fell very sick. Many doctors were called. "Bring her the loveliest rose. It is the symbol of the purest and brightest love on earth," said all. The queen's courtiers searched the entire earth but could not find any such rose.

Meanwhile, the queen's health only worsened day by day and she neared her end.

Then one day, the queen's little son showed her a book that he had just read. He read out the lines from the book and said, "Mother, here is the man whose love was so great that he suffered death to save mankind." A rosy hue spread across the queen's cheeks as she listened to the lines. As soon as she laid her eyes on the book, she saw the vision of Jesus springing forth like a red rose.

## 25 The Top and the Ball

A whipping top and a ball were kept in a small box. The ball was made of expensive leather and was multicoloured while the whipping top was made of ordinary wood. The whipping top loved the ball and hoped to marry it one day.

The ball was very proud of its looks. She refused to marry the top. One day, a young boy was playing with the ball. While playing, he kicked it so hard that it flew out of sight, never to be found again. The top was heartbroken and very upset. Five years passed but the ball didn't return and the top was alone.

Meanwhile, the top was also painted with different colours and looked beautiful. One day, it fell into a garbage dump where it saw something that looked familiar. It was the ball-tattered and torn!

The ball recognised the top and wanted to marry him. But the top said, "You refused to marry me when I looked bad and ugly. Now I shall do the same."

## 26 How Men Got Fire

Once some American Indians, who lived in a forest, needed a fire. They had seen one before but didn't know how to light one. A rabbit came to their rescue and promised to go to the weasel, who often lit a fire.

One night, the rabbit went to the weasel's house where the weasel and his friends were having a bonfire. He covered his head with a cloth and joined the party. While dancing, the rabbit placed the cloth over the fire. Soon the cloth caught fire, and he ran away with it.

Meanwhile, the weasels understood his trick and chased him. But how could they catch the fast rabbit? They prayed to the rain god to extinguish the fire but the clever rabbit hid himself under a tree.

When the rains stopped, he went to the American Indians and gave them the fire.

## 27 The Boy Who Became a Stone

Elonen lived with his grandmother. One day, he was making a bird snare in his courtyard. Suddenly, a small bird appeared and challenged Elonen to catch it. He quickly finished making the snare and ran behind the bird. After a while, he was able to trap the bird and put it inside a large jar.

One day, while Elonen was away, his greedy grandmother ate up the bird. When Elonen returned home and came to know that his bird had died, he was heartbroken. He ran away from the house. On his way, he came across a stone and asked it to eat him up. The stone was magical and did as it was asked to.

Meanwhile, his grandmother started searching for Elonen everywhere.

One day, while walking past the stone, she heard it say, "Your grandson is inside me." She begged the stone to return her grandson but Elonen remained inside the stone forever.

## 28 The Absent-minded Giant

George was an absent-minded giant. He kept lots of pets but he was so forgetful that he often neglected them. During meals, he would reach for a drink and sip from the goldfish bowl instead. He would push a bread slice between the bars of a cage thinking it was a toast rack. He would flick ash into the poor hamster's cage. The pets were fed up and decided to teach George a lesson. Next day he picked up his long roll of bread. "Aaargh!" he roared, holding out a horrid, scaly rattlesnake. "Ha! Ha! Ha!" He found his pets laughing at him. He looked around the birdcage and saw it was full of bread; the goldfish had hardly any water; and there was ash all over the hamster. George realised his mistake and hung his head in shame. He promised his pets that he would look after them better.

## 29 Last Dream of the Old Oak

There once was an old oak tree that had lived through centuries. He was proud to be called the oldest tree in the world. He often thought how lucky he was to enjoy the beauty of nature for so long while mortals could enjoy it only for a few decades.

The tree looked back at his life and thought about all that he had seen though the ages–the sun, the moon, the seas and all the animals–bright and beautiful.

He had seen famous kings, beautiful queens and lots of fierce wars. But he had a last wish–he wanted to grow taller, touch the clouds, feel the stars, and see the heavens above.

However, when the harsh winter months approached, the tree lost all his leaves and his roots became frail. Then one Christmas morning as church bells rang, the oak tree died. God had heard the oak tree and fulfilled his wish to touch the sky. He brought the oak tree to heaven.

## 30 The Singer and the Dolphin

Arion was a handsome singer who lived in the city of Corinth. One day, Arion was returning with precious jewels, which he had won at a competition, when he met some wicked sailors. "Hand over the jewels and you may go," they said. Arion started to sing, and hearing his voice the pirates fell into a stupor listening to him.

A dolphin too swam up to the ship. "I will carry you on my back to the place you wish to go," it said. When the pirates regained their senses, they spread the rumour that Arion had stolen their goods. Meanwhile, Arion reached Corinth and gathered his own army. He attacked the pirates and won the battle. In memory of this event, a grand statue of Arion and the dolphin was constructed at Corinth. It is still a famous landmark.

# 31 David and Goliath

David was a brave shepherd boy. At one time his country was at war. His three older brothers had joined the army to fight against the enemy.

One day, David's father asked him to go and meet his brothers. David went to the place where his country's army had set up camp. The enemy camp was also nearby. Suddenly, he saw a giant shouting very loudly at a distance. He was almost roaring like a lion.

David's brothers told him that the giant was Goliath, an enemy soldier. Every day he would dare them to fight, but nobody was brave enough to fight him.

David declared, "I will fight with Goliath." He went to his king to ask for permission. The king said, "How will you fight such a big giant? You are only a boy." David replied, "I will defeat him because God is with me." The king gave him permission to fight and also asked him to wear enough armour to save himself from the giant. "That will only be a burden for me," said David. "My sling and five smooth stones are enough for me." David came face-to-face with Goliath. Goliath was angry to see that a small boy had come to fight him. But before Goliath could attack him, David hurled a stone at him with his sling. The stone hit Goliath's forehead and he fell to the ground. Then David killed Goliath with his own sword.

Soon, the army of David's country was able to defeat the enemy.

# Contents

*The Story of the Month:   Aladdin*

The Story of the Month
# Aladdin

# Aladdin

Once there lived a poor widow and her son, Aladdin. One day, Aladdin's uncle, Mustafa, came to visit them. He said, "Sister, why don't you let Aladdin come and work for me?" They agreed and Mustafa took Aladdin along with him. They walked in the desert and came to a cave. The cave was full of riches and treasures but Mustafa was afraid to go inside. He wanted Aladdin to go in and get him the treasures instead. "Go inside," commanded Mustafa, "and find me the jewels. You will also find a lamp. Bring it to me."

Aladdin went inside and found more riches than he could ever imagine. He

found a beautiful ring and wore it on his finger. He also collected as many gems as he could, but before he could come out of the cave, Mustafa said, "Quick! Just hand me all the jewels and the lamp!" Aladdin refused. Angry at the refusal, his cruel uncle blocked the entrance of the cave and left.

Aladdin sat in the dark and cried. Then he saw the old lamp and decided to light it. While cleaning it, he rubbed the lamp and out came a genie! "Master, I shall grant you three wishes," he said. Aladdin said, "Take me home!" In seconds,

Aladdin was with his mother, counting the gems he had brought from the cave. Aladdin also brought the ring along with him and when he rubbed it, out came another genie! "Master, I shall grant you three wishes!" said the genie. "Make us rich and happy!" said Aladdin. And Aladdin and his mother lived happily.

One day, Aladdin saw the sultan's daughter and fell in love with her. He went to the palace with gems and asked for her hand in marriage. The king agreed to this. After marriage,

Aladdin showered the princess with all the riches and gave her a huge palace to live in. When the sultan died, Aladdin ruled the kingdom. He was just and kind hearted and everybody was happy under his rule.

Meanwhile, Mustafa came to know how Aladdin found the magic lamp and became rich. He wanted to take the lamp back. So, one day, when Aladdin was away, Mustafa came to the palace dressed as a trader. He cried out, "Get new lamps for old ones! New lamps for old!" Hearing this, the princess took out the magic lamp and gave it to

him. She did not know that the old lamp was indeed magical. She bought a shiny new lamp instead. Mustafa gladly took the lamp and went away. He then commanded the genie, "Send Aladdin's entire palace into the deserts in Africa!" And saying this, Mustafa, along with the princess in the palace, were sent to Africa. Aladdin, on coming back, found his wife and house missing. He searched for the palace for three long days. Finally, he rubbed his magic ring and asked the genie, "Please take me to my princess!" The genie agreed. When he met his

wife, Aladdin and the princess decided to trick Mustafa.

One night, the princess said to Mustafa, "I don't think Aladdin will ever find me here! I might as well live as your slave for I am certain he is dead now!" Mustafa was very happy and ordered for a feast. During the feast, the princess got Mustafa drunk and he fell into a deep sleep.

In the meantime, the princess took the magic lamp to Aladdin. Together, they asked the genie of the lamp to take the entire palace back to Aladdin's kingdom. The genie then killed Mustafa and Aladdin and the princess lived happily ever after.

## 1 Are the Stars Stuck to the Sky?

All the children would go to sleep at night only when Sleep Imp flew over their houses and sang melodious lullabies to them. On a Saturday night, none of the children had gone to sleep because Sleep Imp was late. All the mothers were very angry and finally, one of the mothers went to Sleep Imp to complain about the delay.

Sleep Imp apologised for the delay and said, "I am sorry. I'm late because I had to do so much work. I had to do all the cleaning for tomorrow. Tomorrow is Sunday, a holiday, and everything has to look clean and tidy and pretty. I still have a lot of things to do tonight."

The mother asked, "What things?" Sleep Imp replied, "I have to bring down the bells and polish them so that they can ring loud and clear. Then, I have to go to the gardens and check whether the wind has blown the dust from the grass and the flowers. Then, I have to go up to the sky, bring down the stars and make them shiny and bright and then put them back in their place." The mother demanded, "But the stars are stuck in the sky. How can you take them out?" Sleep Imp was angry on hearing this. He said, "I know what I am doing."

The mother wanted to prove her point but when she peeped through the window she saw that her child was already fast asleep. So there was no point in arguing further with Sleep Imp and she went back. She never found out if at all the stars are stuck in the sky or not.

What do you think?

## 2 The Happy Prince

High above the city stood the statue of a prince, which was gilded with gold. For eyes he had two bright sapphires and a red ruby glowed on his sword hilt. One night, a swallow came to rest on the feet of the statue. The prince said to the swallow, "Will you give the ruby in my sword hilt to the woman living there as her little boy is very ill." The woman sewed for a living. The swallow reached the poor woman's house and laid the ruby beside her thimble. The prince asked the swallow to give one of his sapphire eyes to a man who was feeling cold. Then he asked the swallow to give his other eye to a poor girl who was hungry and had not eaten for days. He told the swallow to take off all his gold and give it to the poor.

In winter, the swallow died and soon the leaden heart of the prince broke and the statue fell down. When God asked his angels to bring him the two most precious things, they brought the leaden heart and the dead bird.

## 3 The Carabao and the Snail

Once there was a carabao. One day, the carabao went to a river where he met a snail. He mocked at the snail and said, "You are so slow." The snail replied, "No, I am not. I can easily beat you in a race." The surprised carabao said, "Let's race and see who beats whom." Soon the race began. The carabao was fast. He covered a long distance and soon the snail was nowhere to be seen. So he called out, "Hey, Snail! Where are you?" Another snail, which was nearby, thought that the carabao was calling him, answered, "Here I am." The carabao was surprised that the snail could run as fast. He started running faster. Every time he stopped to call, some other snail answered him. So he kept on running until he dropped dead.

## 4 The King of the Lake

A very brave warrior one day decided to go out to look for adventure. Soon, he came to a lake with a bridge over it. On the bridge was a snake, as big as a tree. But the fearless warrior crossed the river by jumping over the snake. Suddenly, the snake took the form of a man. He was the king of the lake.

The king declared, "I have been waiting for a warrior brave enough to face the fierce snake that I had become. I will take you to my kingdom where you will have to perform a task for me."

The brave warrior agreed and went with the king. The water of the lake parted to make way for them and they went into the water. When they reached the lake kingdom, they found a huge dragon with eyes of fire and a flaming tongue. The king told the warrior to kill the dragon. The warrior aimed a shot at the dragon's fiery eyes and killed it. The king rewarded him with gold.

## 5 The Treasure

A prince learnt magic, with great effort, so that he could dig and find a treasure.

One day, with his magic, the prince found a treasure on the bank of the river Gianquadara, in Italy. He decided to dig the treasure out. For that the prince needed to make ten billion ants cross the river one by one, on a small boat made of half a shell of a nut.

The prince quickly found a nutshell. He also found an anthill with millions of ants inside it. The prince put one ant on the shell and made it cross the river. Then he put the second, then the third and then the fourth.

What happened next? We can only know that when all the ants have finished crossing the river!

## 6 The Clever Shepherd

Long, long ago there used to live a princess who never laughed. The king declared he would reward anyone who could make her laugh.

A shepherd had a ring that could make people sneeze. He took it to the king. The king put on the ring and started sneezing continuously. Looking at her father, the princess started laughing. The king was furious and took away the ring and imprisoned the shepherd.

One day, the shepherd escaped into the forest. There he saw a strange fig tree with black figs and white figs. When he ate the black figs, two horns grew on his head, which disappeared on eating the white figs. An idea struck the shepherd.

He disguised himself and gave the black figs to the king. As soon as the king ate the figs, two horns grew on his head. The king was frightened and begged for help. The shepherd gave him the white figs in return for his ring and his reward.

# 7 The Evil Cook

Queen Matilda had no children. She was very unhappy and prayed to God. Soon God answered her prayers and blessed her with a son and said that whatever he wished for would be granted.

One day, when the queen was asleep, the wicked cook took the child away from the sleeping queen. "Sire, the queen has allowed the wild beasts to take the child away!" he told the king. As proof, he put hen's blood on the queen's apron. The king was furious. "You deserve to be punished for such a cruel deed. How can a mother neglect her child? You will live in the high tower without any food or water!" proclaimed the king to the queen. But God sent two angels who brought food for her twice a day.

Soon the king's son grew up. "I Wish for a palace and a pretty maiden as a companion," said the boy to the cook. Fearing that the prince might wish to be with his father one day and thus his wicked deed would be exposed, the cook told the maiden to kill the boy in his sleep. But the girl could not kill an innocent boy. She told the boy about the cook's evil plan. The boy cursed him and turned him into a black poodle.

He set out in search of his mother. After finding her he declared, "Mother, I will go to Father and tell him the truth." He presented himself at the king's court the next day and told him about the cook's treachery. The king begged for forgiveness and ordered, "Throw the cook into the deepest, darkest dungeon! He shall never see light again." The three lived in happiness thereafter.

# 8 Salt and Water

Once, a king asked his three daughters, how much they loved him. The first daughter said, "I love you as much as my eyes." The second daughter said, "I love you as much as my heart." The king was very happy to hear this and rewarded the daughters for loving him so much. But when the third daughter said, "I love you as much as salt and water," the king was so angry that he ordered his men to throw her out of the kingdom.

The princess went to live in another kingdom. Meanwhile, the prince of that kingdom fell in love with her and asked her to marry him. The princess invited her father to the wedding. During the dinner, she ordered that the food be served to her father without salt and water. All the guests enjoyed the feast but the princess's father could hardly eat. Then the princess went to him and said, "Do you realize the importance of salt and water?" The king realised his mistake and asked to be forgiven for punishing her.

## 9 The Lion's Share

One day a lion went hunting with a fox, a jackal and a wolf in the forest. After hunting for a long time, they killed a stag.

Now the question arose as to how the game would be divided among the four. The lion was very clever and ordered, "Divide the stag into four parts. The first part is mine as I am the king of the jungle, the second is also mine since I am the judge in this case and the third should also be given to me for my part in the chase. The last part is for you both. You can share it equally" He challenged them to try and claim their part. Frightened of the lion's might, the others didn't dare.

The fox was very disappointed and grudgingly said to himself, "One may help the great in their mission but cannot claim to get an equal share."

## 10 The Man with the Coconuts

One day, a man went to gather coconuts. After gathering many coconuts, he loaded them on his donkey and started walking back home.

On the way, he met a boy and asked him, "How long will I take to reach home?" The boy looked at the heavy burden on the donkey and said, "If you go slowly, you will reach early but if you go very fast, you will be late."

The man was annoyed at the strange reply. He wanted to reach home early and hurried his donkey. As soon as the donkey started moving fast, all the coconuts fell down. The man took a lot of time loading the coconuts again. Every time he hurried his donkey, the coconuts fell and he had to load them again. In the end, he reached home very late since he had tried to hurry each time. He realised what the boy had meant.

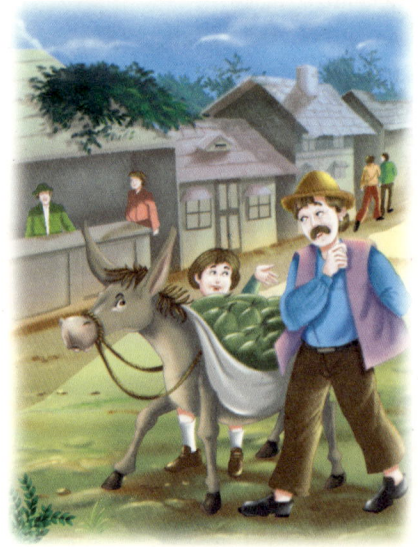

## 11 The One-Eyed Doe

Once a doe used to graze on a cliff by the sea. One day, she became blind in one eye. After that, she always grazed in such a way that her blind eye was towards the sea. With the other eye that was towards land, she kept a watch for hunters. One day, some hunters came in a boat and shot her. This story proves the saying, "You can't escape your fate."

# 12 Noddy and the Naughty Golliwog

Noddy was a little wooden boy whose head bobbed up and down as he walked. One morning he said to his car, "You look dirty! I'll have to give you a wash."

"Mind you wash behind its ears," said a cheeky little voice. Noddy saw a small golliwog behind him. "Cars don't have ears," said Noddy crossly. "Of course, they do. They're under its bonnet. That's where my mother's ears are—under her bonnet," giggled Golliwog. Noddy was sure his car did not have ears even if it did have a bonnet. But he just said, "Go away, and let me wash my car."

"When are you going to clean its teeth and brush its hair?" continued the cheeky golliwog. "I'll wash *your* face and clean *your* teeth first," said Noddy and turned the hose towards the golliwog. The water splashed the little golliwog's face and he ran down the street howling.

# 13 The Piggy Bank

A piggy bank stood on the top-most shelf in the playroom. It was made of shiny porcelain and was so full of coins that it did not rattle.

All the other toys thought that the piggy bank was very rich and respected it for its wealth. The doll always sang lovely songs so that the piggy bank would notice her. The tin soldiers marched up and down in front of the piggy bank to protect it from being robbed.

One day, the little boy who owned the piggy bank brought another coin and put it in. But the piggy bank was so full that as another coin was pushed into it, it broke into pieces and fell on the floor. Somebody came and picked up all the coins.

Soon, another piggy bank was brought and placed on the topmost shelf. The new piggy bank did not rattle either, as it was empty!

## 14 The Admonitions

Once a man went to another town to work. After working for some years, he decided to return to his wife and son. Before leaving, his master said, "I will give you two admonitions that will help you—never change your ways, and think before you act."

The man set out for his hometown. On the way fellow travellers asked, "We are going to take another route, will you come with us?" The man remembered the first admonition and refused to join them. Later, he heard that they were robbed. When he reached home, he was surprised to see his wife dining with a young man. Thinking that his wife had remarried, he wanted to kill them both. But he remembered the second admonition and hid behind the curtains to find out the truth. He heard his wife say to the young man, "Son, let's pray for your father."

He realised his mistake and was happily reunited with his family.

## 15 The Rose and the Amaranth

Once, a rose and an amaranth grew side by side in a beautiful garden. Whoever passed by the garden never missed glancing at the rose and always stopped by and admired it for a moment. One day, looking at the rose blossom in beauty and its sweet fragrance, the amaranth said to it, "I envy your beauty and sweet scent. No wonder everyone admires you." The rose replied sadly, "You only see my beauty. But I live for such a short time since my petals wither away and fall. And then I have no life. But you live forever and never fade even after your flowers are cut. So don't envy me, my dear friend, but be happy with what you are."

All things have to live with their own share of problems, which we may not be aware of. We should learn to be content with what we have.

# 16 Robin Redbreast

One year the winter was very cold. There was thick snow on the trees.

The poor birds could hardly find anything to eat. All the birds sat together to discuss the problem.

The robin had an idea, "I will go and ask the people who live in those houses to give us some crumbs." Saying so, he went to one of the houses nearby. A man was working in the garden. The robin went and perched very close to him. The other birds were afraid to go near humans, but the robin was brave. When the man saw the friendly robin he brought him a tray full of crumbs. The robin felt very happy and called all the other birds to eat with it. In this way all through the winter, the robin arranged food for the other birds.

When the winter season was over, in order to thank the robin, all the birds gave him a red waistcoat and since then, he came to be known as Robin Redbreast.

# 17 The Thirsty Ant

An ant was passing through a room full of grain. "Oh, it's my lucky day!" she said delightedly. She ate as much as she wanted.

After she had eaten her fill, she felt very thirsty and looked around for water. But there was no water around. The ant thought that she would die of thirst. Suddenly, a drop of water fell near her. She lapped it up quickly. That drop of water was a teardrop that had fallen from the eyes of a weeping girl. "Why do you weep?" the ant asked gently. The girl sobbed and replied, "A giant has imprisoned me in this room. He will release me only on the condition that I separate the wheat, barley, and rye from this huge heap of grain. This job will take me at least a month but the giant wants me to do it in one day, otherwise he will kill me."

"This girl has saved my life," thought the ant. "Wipe your tears. Don't worry for I will help you," she said to the girl. Within a few minutes, she called thousands of her friends. All the ants started working and separated the wheat, barley and rye into three separate heaps. The job was completed in less than a day.

When the giant returned, he was surprised and puzzled to see the work completed in time. He had no other choice but to release the girl. The girl and the ant remained very good friends all their lives.

# 18 Clever Elsie

Clever Elsie was a foolish girl. One day, a man called Hans came to their house and said that he would marry Elsie if she proved that she was really very smart. Elsie was sent to the cellar to fetch beer. While filling the pitcher, she saw an axe above her.

Clever Elsie began weeping loudly. The maid was sent to bring her back. "Why are you weeping?" she asked Elsie. "If I marry Hans and if our child comes to this cellar and if the axe falls on my child then he will die!" sobbed Elsie and wept more and more. Hearing her, the maid too started weeping loudly. The same thing happened with Elsie's parents.

When Hans heard everyone crying and came to enquire what had happened, he heard the story and was convinced of Elsie's cleverness and married her.

After a few days, Clever Elsie went to the field to cut corn. But soon, she felt tired and went off to sleep under a tree.

In the evening, Hans saw her sleeping in the field. He put a fowler's net upon her, which had little bells attached to it. But Clever Elsie still did not wake up.

At night Elsie finally woke up. "Why are bells ringing?" she wondered in alarm. "Who is this person in the net?" she thought wondering whether it really was her. When she knocked on her door and asked if Elsie was inside, the answer was yes. Oh, that meant she was not Elsie! Clever Elsie ran away from the village and was never ever seen again.

# 19 The Star Child

Two woodcutters were passing through a pine forest on a winter day. Suddenly, they saw a bright star falling from heaven. They found it to be a little child. "The poor infant will die. I will take him home," said one. Though poor, he brought up the child with love and care. Ten years passed by. The star child grew up to be a handsome boy with skin like ivory and hair like gold. But he was proud and selfish. One day, he was playing with his friends, when a beggar woman came. "Go away! You are ugly." said the boy throwing stones at her. When the woodcutter scolded the boy he replied, "Don't shout at me! You are not my father." The beggar heard their story in amazement and cried, "You are the son I lost in the forest years ago." "How can an ugly woman be my mother?" exclaimed the boy running away into the forest. He sat down beside a pond. Lo! When he looked in the water he saw that he had become as ugly as a toad! His cruelty has transformed his beauty into ugliness.

## 20 The Cold Snowman

Peter peeped out of the window and exclaimed in delight, "Oh, it's snowed last night!" He called all his friends. "Let's build a snowman." They gave the snowman a grand old hat and gloves. Soon, the children left. "Brrrr . . ." the snowman grew cold. Silly, the little Elf felt sorry. Suddenly, an idea struck him. "Bonfire!" he yelled. He took the snowman as close to the fire as he could. "It's so nice he-e-e-re . . ." said the snowman his hat slipping to one side and his buttons popping. But he was so cozy he soon went off to sleep, as did little elf.

"Sizzle-sizzle." Hearing the sound, the elf jumped up to find the snowman gone. Only his hat, scarf and gloves remained. "Snowman, where are you?" he cried. He looked high and low. He hunted everywhere but of course did not find Snowman.

## 21 The Skilful Girl

Once there was an orphan girl. A poor old woman gave her shelter in her house. "She is so kind and thoughtful. I should repay her in some way," thought the grateful girl.

She took some flax and made it into fine thread. Then she wove a very soft cloth. "Please sell this cloth in the market. The money will help you," she said. The old woman thought that the cloth was too fine to sell, so she took it to the king as a gift.

The king was very pleased and gave her a big reward in return.

The king wanted to get the cloth sewn but there was not a tailor in the kingdom that could sew such a fine cloth. "Sire, let the person who has woven this cloth sew it too." Saying this the old woman took the cloth back to the girl. The next day, the girl herself took the garment to the king. Charmed by her beauty and the exquisite garment the king asked her to marry him and they lived happily ever after.

## 22 The Friend's Pot

A woman once borrowed a pot from her friend. The next day, she returned the pot and a smaller pot along with it.

Her friend was very surprised. When she asked her where the small pot had come from, the woman replied, "Your pot gave birth to a baby pot." The friend thought the woman was foolish but was happy to have another pot so she did not say anything.

After some days, the woman borrowed the pot from her friend again. This time she did not return it. When the friend asked her to return the pot she said, "Your pot has died." The friend was surprised, "How can a pot die?" The woman replied, "If it can give birth it can also die." The friend had no choice but to let go of her pot.

## 23 The King Who Wanted a Beautiful Wife

A king wanted to marry a maiden as fair and bright as daylight. He ordered his servant to find such a maiden.

Searching high and low, finally the servant arrived at a small house. An old woman, who used to spin wool, lived there. The servant knocked at the door and asked for some water. The old woman handed out a pitcher through a hole in the door. With all the spinning, her hands had become soft and white. When the servant saw them, he thought that she must be a very beautiful maiden to have such soft and gentle hands. He took her to the king.

The old woman put a thick veil and went to the palace. When she removed her veil, the king was surprised to see such an old ugly woman. He threw her out of the palace. A fairy took pity on the old woman and made her young again. In the morning when the king saw her, he fell in love with her and married her.

# 24 Gulliver in Brobdingnag

After escaping from Lilliput, Gulliver returned to England. After a few days he set off on his voyages once again. After some time the *adventure* was blown off-course by a storm and cast ashore in a new country.

Gulliver became busy exploring the new surroundings and found himself in a corn-field. He realised that he was lost. Finally, a 72 feet tall farmer found Gulliver and took him home. "Where am I?" asked Gulliver. "You are in Brobdingnag, the land of giants," replied the farmer. "You are so tiny, you will make a good pet for my daughter. She will be very happy," he said.

The farmer's daughter adored Gulliver and kept him with her throughout his stay. She treated him like a play-thing, dressing and teaching him. One day the farmer decided to make some money and toured with Gulliver all over the country. Poor little Gulliver had to perform as many as ten times a day! Finally the farmer sold him to the king of Brobdingnag.

Gulliver spent two years in Brobdingnag. But poor Gulliver's woes did not end here. Once barrel-sized apples fell on him, nearly squashing him to death and another time hailstones as big as tennis balls, left him hurt all over with bruises.

Then, one day, on a visit to the seashore, an eagle snatched up the box in which Gulliver was being kept and dropped it in the sea. The sailors on a passing ship picked up the box and Gulliver was very happy to be back home where he was no longer considered a midget.

# 25 Crab the Merchant

The king had lost a precious ring! He declared that he would reward anyone who found it for him.

A clever peasant, named Crab, went to the king and said, "I am an astrologer and will find your ring." The king told his servants to take Crab to a room and treat him well. As the days passed by, Crab pretended that he knew astrology and pored over books. The servants were very afraid of him. One day, Crab asked his wife to hide in the room and say, "He is the one!" when any servant entered. When one of the servants heard the voice saying, "He is the one," he was scared and confessed of stealing the ring. He offered Crab money and begged him to leave him alone. Crab asked him to put the ring in the mouth of a turkey in the garden. Then Crab went to the king and declared that a turkey had swallowed the ring. When the turkey was cut, the ring was found. The king rewarded Crab handsomely.

## 26 The Two Crows

Two crows decided to have a competition to see who could carry a bag to a greater height in the sky. Each crow was free to choose what to fill in his bag.

Two bags of same size were arranged. The first crow filled it with cotton as he thought it would be the lightest thing to carry. He made fun of the second crow who filled his bag with salt, which was quite heavy. Soon, many birds and animals arrived to watch the competition.

The competition was about to begin when it started to rain. The second crow had expected this. Soon the rain dissolved the salt in his bag and he easily carried it to a greater height. However, the cotton in the first crow's bag absorbed water and it became so heavy that he couldn't even get off the ground and had to admit defeat.

## 27 The Jumping Competition

Once upon a time, a cricket, a frog and a kangaroo decided to have a jumping competition.

The king and his daughter, the lovely princess, came to know about the competition and promised a reward for the one who would jump the highest. The cricket jumped high. He was the one who jumped the highest. He jumped so high that no one ever saw him land. So, the judges disqualified him. The frog was bigger than the cricket. And when he jumped, the people saw him. But sadly, the frog landed right on top of the king's head! The frog was also out of the competition. The clever kangaroo jumped straight into the princess's lap! She was very happy with him and the kangaroo won the competition. The king, as promised, rewarded the kangaroo with many gifts.

## 28 The Little Omelette

Once there was a little woman who had a little hen that laid little eggs. She used to make omelettes with the eggs.

One day, a fly came and ate up her omelettes. The woman went to the magistrate for some help. He gave her a club to hit the fly. Just then, a fly sat on the magistrate's nose and she hit it with the club. The fly flew away but the magistrate's nose broke.

## 29  The Clever Peasant

A king went to visit a village. He asked a peasant, "How much do you earn in a day?" The peasant replied, "I earn four ounces." The king said, "What do you do with them?" The peasant replied, "The first I eat, the second one I put on interest, the third I give back and the fourth I throw away."

The king was surprised and asked the peasant for an explanation. The peasant replied. "With the first ounce I feed myself. With the second one, I feed my children so that they take care of me when I get old and I get my interest. With the third one, I feed my father and repay what he has done for me when I was a child. With the fourth one, I feed my wife, which is as good as throwing it away because I don't get any profit."

The king was impressed and rewarded the peasant.

## 30  Pepper Corn

An old man lived with his wife. They had no children and were very unhappy.

One day, the old woman went to the garden to pick beans. She looked at the beans and sighed, "I wish you were my children." And lo! Her wish came true. "I don't know what to do with so many children. I wish all but one would turn into beans." Again, her wish came true. She took the little child home and named him Pepper Corn. Everybody loved him.

One day, Pepper Corn fell into boiling soup and died. The old man and woman were heartbroken and started weeping, "Pepper Corn has died." When the dove heard this she pulled out her feathers, the apple tree shook off its apples, and the well emptied out all its water to mourn his death. Pepper Corn would never be forgotten.

# Contents

*The Story of the Month:   The Tin Soldier*

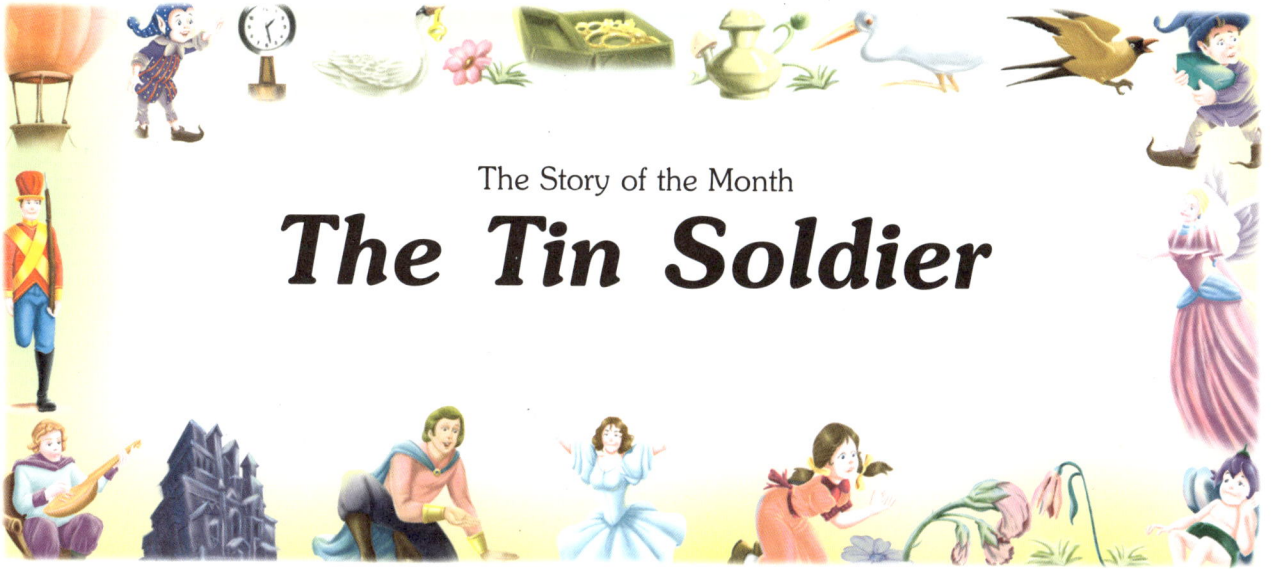

The Story of the Month

# The Tin Soldier

## The Tin Soldier

Once a little boy was given a birthday present of a set of twenty-five tin soldiers. All the soldiers had shiny red and blue uniforms and gleaming tin muskets.

However, one of the soldiers stood out from the rest because he had only one leg. In the same nursery there were many other toys. There were wax puppets and jack-in-the-boxes. There were playing cards and porcelain dolls. There were colour pencils and bouncing balls. There also lived a beautiful, dancing ballerina doll who stood at the entrance to a cardboard castle which had a small mirror for a lake in front of it.

She balanced herself on one leg so well that the tin soldier thought that she had only one leg. She wore a blue dress with a scarf. The scarf had a tinsel rose pinned on it in the centre. The tin soldier admired the ballerina from a distance and soon fell in love with her. "But she is so beautiful and she lives in a beautiful castle! She will not like me at all!" thought the poor tin soldier and felt very sad.

A goblin, who also lived in the same nursery, did not like the tin soldier at all. He was jealous of the tin soldier whenever the ballerina smiled at him. The ballerina really liked the one-legged tin

soldier in his smart red uniform.

One day, the goblin warned the tin soldier, "You better stay away from the ballerina! She is mine! I am warning you!" But the tin soldier loved the ballerina so much that he just couldn't stop admiring her.

One day, the puppets were playing together and the ballerina was dancing prettily. It was raining heavily outside. The tin soldier was standing on the windowsill and watching the dancing doll. The window was open. The angry goblin crept behind the tin soldier and pushed him out of

the window. Two boys, who were passing by found him on the street and floated him down a gutter in a paper boat. The little tin soldier flowed away in the water, into the drain nearby. He was heartbroken because he feared he would never see his ballerina ever again.

He saw a huge rat but the tin soldier was brave and holding onto his musket he floated away just in time and escaped. In the dark drain, the poor one-legged tin soldier had to fight many rats. The drain led into a canal where the water swirled fiercely, and here the little paper boat was torn. A fish

saw the tin soldier and swallowed him. He lay inside the fish for three days, in the dark.

The tin soldier thought that he would die inside the fish. One day, a fishermen caught the fish and sold it in the market. A lady bought the fish from the market. Now this lady happened to be the little boy's mother. Soon, the fish was being prepared for dinner in their kitchen. When the cook cut the fish, she found the tin soldier. Exclaiming in wonder, she called the boy and gave him the tin soldier.

The tin soldier was very happy to be back in the same house with the same toys! He saw his beautiful ballerina dancing at the end of the table, while he stood at the other end.

But alas! The naughty little boy did not like the tin soldier anymore and he threw the poor tin soldier into the fireplace. Suddenly, there was a gush of strong, cold wind which blew the ballerina as well, into the fire. The tin soldier and the ballerina melted in the fire. The next morning, when a maid cleaned the fireplace of the ashes, she found a tiny red tin heart and tiny red rose. These belonged to the tin soldier and the ballerina, who were finally together.

# 1 The Singing Bone

A boar was causing a lot of destruction. The king announced that whoever could free the country of the wild beast would win his daughter's hand in marriage. Two brothers—one shrewd and the other innocent—decided to kill the boar.

The younger brother was sincere and tried to think of ways to kill the boar. One day, he met a quaint little man in the forest who told him, "Take this black spear. Attack the beast with it." He did as told and killed the animal.

Meanwhile, the older brother was drinking and making merry, confident that he would kill the boar easily. But when he saw his younger brother carrying the dead boar, he was very jealous. He took his brother to a bridge and pushed him off. He then told the king that he had killed the boar, and won his daughter's hand as reward.

But evil deeds do not remain hidden. Years later, a shepherd, while crossing that bridge, found a bone and began to blow it. At once the bone started singing,

"Ah friend thou blowest upon my bone.
Long have I lain beside the water,
My brother slew me for the boar,
And took for his wife the king's young daughter."

The shepherd took the bone to the king and it sang the same song over and over again. The king realized what had happened and the older brother's treachery was revealed to all. He was put in a sack and drowned as punishment.

# 2 The Wonderful Veil

A farmer lived in a hut near the woods. Though he was poor, he was very happy because the beauty of nature around him was more precious to him then wealth.

One day, the farmer smelled a sweet fragrance coming from the woods. He followed it and saw a beautiful veil caught in the branches of a tree. The veil was more beautiful than anything he had ever seen before. It was woven with sunlight and moonbeams and studded all over with stars. But the moment he removed the veil from the tree, a fairy appeared and said, "This veil belongs to me! I can't go to fairyland without it. Please give it back to me." The farmer said, "You can have your veil but you will have to dance for me the way only fairies know how to."

The fairy agreed and danced with the veil swirling around her. Thousands of flowers fell from the veil and the farmer was happier than ever before.

# 3 The Ass in the Lion's Skin

There was once a mischievous ass who put on a lion's skin. He went off towards the forest trying to scare all the foolish animals he saw.

The ass was highly amused to see the others run away from him in fear. He continued enjoying himself in this manner for a few days. Everyone in the forest talked about the lion but the poor animals were helpless because of their fear.

One day, the ass came across a fox and tried to frighten him as well. But the clever fox soon heard the ass's real voice. He laughed and exclaimed, "You silly ass. I too would have been frightened like the others if I had not heard you bray. Didn't you realise that you would be caught soon?" The fox was too smart to be fooled by outward appearances.

# 4 The Story of a Monkey

A thorn was once stuck to the tail of a mischievous monkey. It went to a barber and asked him to remove the thorn. While removing the thorn with his razor, the barber cut the monkey's tail. The monkey was very angry and said, "Either put back my tail or give me your razor." The poor barber gave the monkey his razor.

On its way back, the monkey met a woman cutting wood and said, "Use my razor. You will be able to cut the wood easily." The woman did but broke the razor. The monkey said, "Either return my razor or give me your wood." The old woman gave the wood. At some distance the monkey met another woman baking cakes. The monkey said to her, "Use my wood to bake more cakes." The woman was very happy but then the monkey said, "Either return my wood or give me the cakes." The woman had to give up the cakes.

But alas! Before the monkey could eat the cakes, a dog snatched them away.

## 5 Jack and His Goat

Jack lived with his poor parents. One day he set out to earn money. He took his goat with him.

After a while, he came to a town where he sold the goat to a merchant. The merchant placed the goat in a yard where he kept all his other animals. At night, Jack went and stole his goat. Now he had both the goat and the money.

After a few days, Jack returned home. His parents were happy to see the money, but when they came to know that Jack had stolen his goat and cheated the merchant, they were very angry. Jack's father said, "This goat will bring you misfortune." After some days, Jack again set out to earn some money. On the way a robber killed him and took away his goat.

## 6 The Magic Bottle

Mick was a poor farmer. One day, he decided to go to the fair to sell his cow. On the way, he met a dwarf who gave him a magic bottle in exchange for the cow. With the help of the wish-fulfilling bottle, Mick became very rich.

When Mick's landlord came to know the secret of Mick's wealth, he forcefully took his bottle away. Mick became poor again and was ultimately left with only a cow. He decided to sell it. On his way to the fair he again met the dwarf. This time the dwarf gave him another magic bottle from which, when Mick made a wish two men came out and started beating him until he ordered them to stop. Mick took the bottle to his landlord and said, "This bottle is better than the first." When the landlord made a wish, the two men came out and started beating him. Mick ordered them to stop only when the landlord agreed to return the first bottle.

Mick happily took the two bottles home.

# 7 The Three Feathers

A king had three sons. Two sons were clever but the third one was so simple that he was called Simpleton. One day the king said, "The one who brings me the most beautiful carpet shall inherit my kingdom. I shall fly three feathers and you must follow their directions to search for the carpet!" Saying this, he flew three feathers in the air. One son went East and the other, West. But Simpleton remained there. His feather fell on the floor. He saw a trap door beneath the feather and went inside. Simpleton saw a fat toad sitting along with other smaller toads. The toad asked, "What do you want?" He replied, "I want the prettiest carpet in the world!" And the toad gave him a pretty carpet. Simpleton took it to the king and he was made king.

Simpleton's brothers were jealous and they said, "Father! Simpleton is too simple to rule the kingdom!" The king said, "The one who brings me the most beautiful ring shall inherit my kingdom!" Now, the toad gave Simpleton the prettiest ring in the world. Simpleton's brothers cried, "Father! Simpleton is too simple to rule!" So the king said, "Bring me the most beautiful woman and you shall inherit my kingdom!"

This time, the toad changed a little toad into a lovely maiden and sent her with Simpleton. The brothers came back with peasant wives. They said, "Father, let's see whose wife is strongest! The lady who jumps through this ring in the centre of the hall will get the kingdom!" Simpleton's wife leapt like a deer, while the other ladies broke their legs! Simpleton inherited the kingdom and lived happily ever after.

# 8 The Last Pearl

Once a beautiful newborn baby girl lay in a room.

The guardian angel of the house and the good angel of the baby watched as the fairies of health, wealth, and love came and gave their pearls as gifts to the newborn baby and blessed the child. The baby had been blessed with everything it could ever want—good health, wealth and love.

The guardian angel said, "All the fairies have come, but one fairy remains." The good angel asked, "Who is it? Let us go to her and ask her to give her pearl."

The guardian angel took the good angel to a house in which lay a dead woman. Her family was in sorrow. The angels went to a fairy sitting in the corner of the room.

The guardian angel said to the good angel, "This is the fairy who is yet to give the last pearl. She is the fairy of sorrow.

"The gift of sorrow gives meaning to the other gifts of life."

# 9 The Gold Crown

Robin the fairy was very sad. Two big tears rolled down his cheeks. "Oh, dear! What's the matter?" asked Butterfly. "I'm sad because I can't do the things the other fairies can," said Robin. "I can't paint the sunset pink or hang dew drops on grasses," he moaned. "Every year the king gives little silver crowns to fairies who do beautiful work," he continued. "And I never win one," he wailed.

"Cheer up," said Butterfly. "Why don't you go to the world of boys and girls and help there." "Good idea!" said Robin and wiped his tears and flew out of Fairyland.

He saw Mr. Wind tugging at a pretty frock on a clothesline. He sat on the frock and held on to it till an old woman came out and thanked him for not letting the wind blow away her clean clothes. Next he saw a little boy crying because his balloon had flown away. Off flew Robin into the sky and brought down the balloon. "Thank you, little fairy," smiled the boy gratefully. Robin was very happy. "I won't mind not winning a crown anymore," he said. "I've found something I *can* do and it makes me happy."

Next day, the king held his court and he gave out many silver crowns to all the fairies who had done good work. At the end, he brought out a gold crown. "This is for the fairy who went to the world of boys and girls and did beautiful things there. We are all very proud of him."

You can imagine Robin's surprise when he got the silver coin He was very happy and hugged Butterfly.

# 10 The Man from the Sky

There was a man who was always fooling others. One day, he met a lady. She asked him, "Who are you?" He said, "Don't you know me? I have come from the sky!"

She believed him and happily asked him if he had met her husband who had died recently. He answered, "Oh, I meet him all the time! But madam, he is in a very bad condition!" The lady was worried. "What happened to my husband?" she asked. The man replied, "He has not found a job and cannot earn a living. So he has no money and is very poor!"

The lady agreed to pack some food and clothes for her husband to send along with this man from the sky. But he said, "No! They won't allow that and I will be caught and punished for doing so. However, I can sneak in some money and give it to him if you want!" Saying this, he tricked the foolish woman and walked away with all her money.

# 11 The Naughty Clock Winder

The king of Elfland had a large collection of clocks. An elf called Dickory Dock had to wind them up every day. Dickory Dock was a forgetful elf. So the king gave Dickory Dock an enchanted key and said, "Now you don't have to use many different keys. You can wind up all the clocks with this key. In fact, it can wind up anything."

Alas! Dickory Dock would still forget to wind the clocks. The furious king punished him severely. The naughty elf decided to teach the king a lesson. He wound up all the furniture in the castle! Soon all the chairs and books were dancing. "Mercy on us! This must be Dickory Dock's doing. Fetch him!" exclaimed the king. He wound Dickory Dock up with the magic key and banished him from the kingdom. And so he goes dancing around to this day.

# 12 Hole in the Water

A handsome and rich man decided to get married but could not find the right girl.

One day, he met a beautiful lady near a well and fell in love with her. He asked her if she would marry him. She replied, "I will marry you but only if you can do one thing. You must make a hole in the water for me!" "That is impossible!" cried the man. She said, "If this is true love, then even miracles can happen." The man walked away sadly. He really did love the woman but didn't know how he could make a hole in the water.

Months passed and soon it was winter. All the lakes and ponds, and the water in the well, froze.

Then the man remembered what the woman had asked for. He quickly ran to the well where he had met her and saw her sitting there. He took a stick and made a hole in the ice. The woman was pleased and agreed to marry him. He married her with a lot of pomp and splendour.

## 13 Flowers from the Moon

Once there lived a handsome prince on a high mountain. He wanted to go to the moon because he loved the gentle moonlight. He loved the moon's gentle white shine.

One day, he fulfilled his dream and really went to the moon. There he met the Moon King's daughter. She was a lovely young princess. They fell in love with each other and wandered together all over the moon among the flowers and danced together.

But soon, it was time to go back to earth and the prince felt very sad. The princess gave him a beautiful flower that grew on the moon, so that the prince could always look at it and remember her.

The prince took the flower, bid the princess goodbye and went all the way back to earth. He planted the flower, and soon it covered all the mountains like a lovely white carpet.

It is believed that this is how the alpine flowers reached the earth from the moon!

## 14 The Big Magic Bird

A poor fisherman was able to catch only a few small fish every day. One day while he was fishing, a big bird came and sat on his boat. It was the magic bird, which helped poor people. The bird promised to bring him a big fish every day.

Soon, the fisherman became rich by selling the fish that the bird brought.

Meanwhile, the king had gone blind. The court physician said that he could only be cured if he washed his eyes with the blood of the magic bird. The king announced that whoever caught the magic bird would get a big reward. When the fisherman heard this, he became greedy. When the bird came the next day, he caught hold of its feet. But the bird was very strong. It flew away with the fisherman hanging from its feet. The fisherman couldn't hold on for very long and fell to the ground and died.

# 15 The White Squash

Once upon a time there lived a poor couple. They were very sad because they had no children. They always prayed to God to bless them with a child.

The couple was so poor that they hardly had much to eat. They lived on the big white squashes that grew in their garden. But one season, the vine stopped bearing fruits. A lot of flowers bloomed on it but they did not turn into fruits.

One day, the woman was very happy to see a small green squash. After a few days, it ripened and they decided to cut it. As they put the knife in a small voice said, "Be careful!" When they carefully cut the squash they found a small boy in it. The couple was very happy.

The woman took the boy and bathed him with water. But to their astonishment, the water turned into gold as soon as it touched the boy. They realized that the boy was special and they were never poor again.

# 16 The Performer and the Flea

Once there was a performer who had trained a flea to perform tricks. He went from place to place with his performing flea to earn money.

One day, they visited a distant country and performed in a king's court. The princess was delighted with the flea's performance and wanted to keep the flea. She was very stubborn and refused to eat food if her wish was not granted. The king forced the performer to give him the flea and gave it to his daughter. The princess was very happy once her wish was fulfilled.

Left with no means of earning a livelihood, the performer was very upset and wanted his flea back but didn't know what to do.

After a lot of thought, he made a plan. He disguised himself and went to the king.

"Sire, I beg permission to make a big cannon for you," he pleaded. The king happily agreed. The performer asked for a piece of silk cloth, some ropes and a basket. But instead of making a cannon he made a big balloon.

The king who had never seen a cannon or a balloon believed the clever performer. The performer told the king that he needed the help of a flea to cool the cannon. The king called for the flea and handed it to the performer.

The clever performer jumped into the balloon and flew away to his country with his flea.

# 17 The Good Brother

Once upon a time three princes set out in search of adventures. The two older brothers made fun of their kind-hearted younger brother, who was called Simon.

On their way, they came across an anthill. The older brothers wanted to destroy it, but Simon would not let them do so. After a while, they wanted to kill the ducks swimming in the lake. Again, Simon stopped them from doing so. A little later, they came to a tree with a big beehive. "Let's build a fire. This will suffocate the bees and we can get their honey," suggested one brother. Again, Simon spoiled their plan.

Finally, the princes reached an enchanted castle. "If you want to deliver the castle from enchantment, you have to perform three tasks. You have to collect a thousand pearls lying below the moss. By sunset, even if one pearl is missing, you will be turned into stone," said the quaint little man at the castle door. "The key to the princess's chamber lies at the bottom of the lake. Once the chamber is open you must pick out the youngest princess." The older brothers failed and were turned into stone.

When it was Simon's turn, the ants he had saved, collected all the pearls. The ducks brought the key of the princess's chamber from the water. The queen of the bees recognised the youngest princess for Simon, by tasting her lips. The princess had had honey before falling asleep.

Simon was very happy. He married the princess and became the king.

# 18 The Farmer and His Sons

There was a rich farmer who had worked hard all his life. But now, he had grown old and was ailing. He was on his deathbed. He wanted to be sure that after his death, his sons would give the same attention to the farm as he had given throughout his life.

He called his sons to his bedside and said, "My sons, I have something important to share with you. There is a great treasure lying hidden in one of my vineyards. If you dig properly, you will find it and will become very rich."

After the farmer's death, the sons started digging every portion of the land. They continued to dig for days and days but did not find the treasure. But their labour did not go in vain. This time the vines produced an abundant crop of high quality and they became rich.

They realised the meaning of the treasure their father had talked about.

Real wealth lies in hard work.

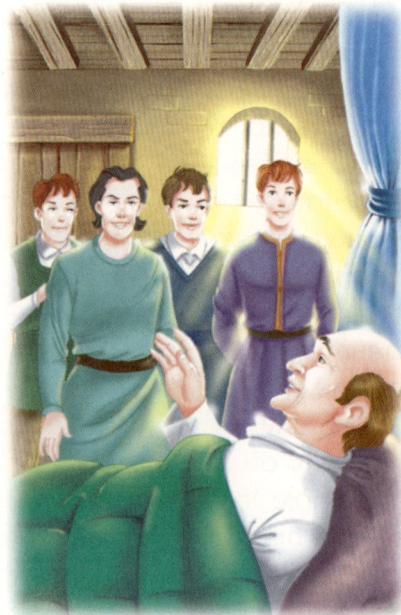

## 19 A Mouse Wedding

Little Johnny was fast asleep when the Sleep Fairy woke him up and said, "Quick! Get dressed! We are going to the mouse's wedding!"

"Whooosh!" The Sleep Fairy turned Johnny into a tiny boy with a touch of her magic wand. He wore a tin soldier's uniform and went for the wedding. "Cheesecakes and cheese candies! Even the walls are made of cheese!" squealed Johnny. Even the bride and the groom sat on a cheese couch. All the guests threw pumpkin seeds at the couple instead of rice. They sang and danced to songs about cheese. Little Johnny enjoyed himself and had a wonderful time all night. "Wake up, dear! Time for school," said Mummy. Little Johnny realised that it had all been a nice dream. Sleep Fairy's little dream.

## 20 The Ice Cream Cart

Anne was a poor girl who lived with her mother. Every day, an ice cream man would pass by her house but she had no money with which to buy one. She would look at other children licking large cones of ice cream and wish she could also be one of them.

One day, the ice cream man took pity on her and gave her the whole ice cream cart. He said, "This is a magic cart. You can ask it to make any kind of ice cream. But when you want it to stop, you must say, 'Enough now'." Anne was very happy; she ate ice cream all day.

One day, while she was away at school, her mother asked the cart to make some ice cream. The cart started doing so. But Anne's mother did not know how to stop it, so the cart went on making ice cream.

Soon, the whole house was filled with ice cream. When Anne returned and saw ice cream everywhere, she had to lick her way to the cart and stop it!

## 21 The Happy Family

Once there lived a snail couple in the woods. They were in search of a pretty snail bride for their only son. The buzzing flies in the forest came to them and said, "There is a beautiful snail, who lives just ten minutes flying distance from here! She will be good for your son!"

The snails agreed and told the girl to visit them. The pretty snail took only eight days to reach them and they were very happy that she was this fast. Their son liked her too. The bees made the wedding cake and the fireflies made the lights. The ants were the bridesmaids. There was lots of rejoicing and merrymaking and the snails were married.

The snail family was finally complete and they lived together happily ever after.

## 22 The Snowdrop

It was a very cold winter and the snowdrop flower seed lay under the snow-covered earth. It was not time for it to break through the earth yet.

One day, a drop of rain reached the sleeping flower. "You should see the magical world above!" it said. Snowdrop wanted to go up even though it was not yet summer. "Let me stretch myself," he thought and grew out above the earth. "Look whose here!" exclaimed the sunbeams happy to see him—he was the first. But soon clouds covered the sun and cold winds began to blow. They said to the snowdrop, "You are too early! You will die." But the flower had faith that the summer would come, so it stood tall and strong in the cold.

Then a girl came and plucked the snowdrop. She said, "It is the first flower!" Snowdrop felt proud.

The girl kept it in a glass of water beside the window in a warm room. And soon, the sunbeams shone on it through the window and summer came.

## 23 Sly's Ice Cream

Sly the Gnome was walking behind Mr. Wisdom, the wise man. "Clink!" A shining one-pound coin fell out of Mr. Wisdom's pocket and rolled down the street. Sly picked it up and slipped it into his pocket. He knew that was stealing, but then he was a mean gnome. Walking on he found a group of children crowding round a man. "Why are you all so excited?" he asked. One of the children said, "Oh, don't you know? It's the ice cream man. Here, try some ice cream." Sly took a bite. "Umm . . ." He loved the sweet delicious taste. "Can I get some for a pound?" he asked. "You can get a whole box for a pound," said the children.

Selfish Sly thought, "I will have it for my tea and won't share it with anyone." He paid for the box of ice cream with Mr. Wisdom's coin and happily whistled as he set off for home.

The day was hot. As Sly walked home, the ice cream began to melt. Slowly it started dripping from a corner of the box. He couldn't understand what was happening. He peered into the box and saw there was no ice cream. In its place was some cold yellow liquid. "Where is my ice cream?" he cried out loud. He thought the ice cream man had cheated him. "I can't eat this," he shouted angrily and flung the box away from him. "Splat!" The box land on Mr. Wisdom who was just turning round the corner! "Oho! I'll teach you some manners, my boy!" said Mr. Wisdom, wiping the ice cream from his face. He grabbed Sly and gave him a good spanking. Crying, Sly ran home promising never to steal again.

## 24 The Two Candles

Once a wax candle and a tallow candle were having a conversation. The wax candle was very vain and boasted, "I will be placed in a silver candle stand at tonight's party." The tallow candle answered, "It is certainly better to be made of wax than of tallow but I am happy that I burn in the kitchen where food is cooked."

Suddenly, a rich lady came and picked up all the candles. Seeing the tallow candle along with the wax candle, the lady gave it to a poor boy who was passing by.

The poor boy took the tallow candle home. Seeing the small cottage, the tallow candle thought, "How lucky the wax candle is to be in its rich home."

Meanwhile, the mother lit the tallow candle. One of the children said, "Oh, we have light in the house today!" The tallow candle saw the joy in his eyes and was happy to be in the cottage and did not envy the wax candle again.

## 25 The Fountain of Youth

An old woodcutter and his wife had spent many happy years together. But now that they were getting old, they were afraid that death would separate them.

One day, the woodcutter went to the forest. He lost his way and came to a fountain. He was very thirsty, so he drank some water from the fountain. But as soon as he did that, he became young again. Now, he just looked twenty years old. He realised that he had found the fountain of youth!

Happily he ran home to his wife, who at first could not recognise him. But when she was told about the fountain she also wanted to be young again and ran to the forest.

The woodcutter followed her to the fountain of youth only to find a baby girl near it. He realised that his wife had drunk too much of the magic water. But he took the baby girl home and brought her up, and they lived happily for many more years.

## 26 The Lute Player

During a war, the enemy captured the king. They asked his queen to pay a ransom if she wanted her husband back.

One day, a lute player came to the enemy king's court and began to play. The king loved the music so much that he said, "You can ask for anything and I shall give it to you!" The lute player said, "Give me the captured king as my slave!" The enemy agreed and king was set free.

Soon, the lute player and the slave king left the palace and after some distance, the lute player set him free. The king returned to his kingdom and said, "When I was a slave the queen did not care! I shall kill her!" Saying this, he marched into his bedroom. But, he heard the strains of beautiful lute music. He then saw his queen playing the lute and understood who the mysterious lute player was.

## 27 The First Monkey

Once there lived an old woman and her grandson in a hut. The old woman worked hard to feed her grandson and herself but her grandson was a lazy boy. He did not help her in her work and took her money and spent it all on his friends.

One day, he came home hungry. "Where is my food?" he demanded. Alas! The food was not ready. He became angry and finding coconuts lying on the ground, threw them at his grandmother. "Food! Food! Food!" he chanted stamping his foot. The good behaviour fairy was passing by. "I'll teach this boy manners!" she thought. She waved her magic wand and whoosh . . . the boy turned into a furry animal with a long tail. When his friends saw him they threw stones at him. Lo! They too turned into animals. The people drove them out of the town.

The boy and his friends then began living on trees and came to be known as monkeys.

## 28 The Coachman's Painting

A coachman who served in the king's palace was also a talented artist. His paintings looked real and alive. Once he painted a portrait of his sister. The painting was so beautiful and life like that he kept it in the royal stable. And whenever he felt sad and lonely, the coachman would talk to the painting. People thought that a woman visited him every night. When the king heard about this he decided to find out the truth for himself. One night, he visited the stable. When he saw the painting, the king fell in love with the beautiful woman. He asked the coachman who it was. He was charmed by the coachman's sister's beauty and married her amidst pomp and splendour. The coachman moved into the palace and they lived happily ever after.

## 29 The Crystal Castle

A prince and princess were in love and about to marry. A wicked magician imprisoned the princess in a crystal castle. "No one can climb up the slippery wall!" declared the magician. "Whoever tries will slip and fall to death."

Heartbroken the prince wandered in the forest. One day, he saved the lives of three fairies. "Take these gifts prince. They may help you in future," said the grateful fairies. The first gift was a cloak with which he could become invisible; the second was a flying horse, while the third was a magic wand that could open any door.

The prince wore the cloak and became invisible. He then sat on the flying horse and crossed the high walls to reach the castle. Using the magic wand, he opened the door of the room in which the princess was imprisoned. He set her free and brought her back. They got married and all the fairies were invited to the wedding.

## 30 The Enchanted Valley

In the Enchanted Valley, during autumn, there was a terrible fire. The people were very troubled.

"Let us go to the powerful magician named Man of Ice. He is sure to help us," said one man. They went to the magician. The great man let down his long flowing hair and swung it vigorously. There were huge gusts of wind followed by rain. But the fire was not put out. The rain turned to snow and still the fire did not stop. "Run! The Man of Ice cannot help us," said the people cursing him. The Man of Ice just shook his head.

In summer, the people of the Enchanted Valley returned. They were amazed to see a lake with sparkling blue lake. This was where the big fire had raged and all the snow had melted. "Look what the Man of Ice has given us!" exclaimed the people. They gave him many gifts as a token of thanks.

# 31 The Little Match Girl

Once there was a little girl who used to make a living by selling matches in the street. It was New Year's Eve and people all around were merrymaking and celebrating.

The little girl was sitting beside a fountain in the freezing cold. She was wearing torn and ragged clothes and had no shoes on her feet. No one had bought her matchboxes that day and she was frightened to go home because she knew her father would scold her for coming back without selling anything. She wanted to light a match to keep herself warm but was scared that her father would scold her for wasting a matchstick. Finally, unable to bear the cold anymore, she took out one matchstick and lit it. Lo! She was sitting in front of a warm stove. She reached out her hands to feel the heart but the fire soon died out. Then she lit another match and saw a dinner table with a roast goose on it. She chuckled in delight but after a while, this match also died out. She looked up at the sky and saw a falling star. Her grandmother used to say, "A falling star is a soul that has reached the sky." When she struck another match she saw her grandmother.

That night, she burnt all her matchsticks, wishing to keep her grandmother with her. Finally, together they flew up to heaven. The next morning, the little match girl lay frozen to death, with a smile on her lips. No one would ever know the wonderful dreams she had had, the previous night.